IRISH ELECTIONS 1918-77

Cornelius O'Leary

IRISH ELECTIONS
1918-77

Parties, voters and proportional
representation

Gill and Macmillan

First published 1979 by
Gill and Macmillan Ltd
15/17 Eden Quay
Dublin 1
with associated companies in
London, New York, Delhi, Hong Kong
Johannesburg, Lagos, Melbourne
Singapore, Tokyo

0 7171 0898 8

Typeset by Joe Healy Typesetting, Dublin
Printed and bound in Great Britain by
Redwood Burn Limited
Trowbridge & Esher

Contents

IN MEMORY OF

JAMES HOGAN

scholar, teacher, friend

Preface

In the early 1950s, as a postgraduate student at University College Cork, I engaged on a comparative study of the electoral systems of Ireland and other European States. Then, in 1959, I was invited by Professor Ferdinand A. Hermens to write the second in a series of studies of national electoral systems, which the University of Notre Dame Press was then publishing under his editorship. The book appeared in 1961 under the title, *The Irish Republic and its Experiment with Proportional Representation*. I am grateful to Professor Hermens for entrusting this task to an unknown research student.

The book covered Dáil elections from the establishment of the Irish Free State to the first referendum on PR, in 1959; it was found useful by students of Irish politics and went out of print in 1975. By then a sequel was clearly needed, but as a general election was in the offing, its preparation was delayed until after the election of June 1977. The original intention was to reproduce the earlier work as it stood, in conjunction with the new material. However, it soon became apparent that this would not be practicable: the space devoted to the last seventeen years was almost as much as was taken up by the previous forty; and the footnotes had also to be revised in the light of more recent psephological studies. So it seemed best to rewrite the whole work, and present it as a new book with a new title.

In this book, using the Dáil general elections as the main object of study, I have tried to provide an analysis of their results which will be intelligible to the general reader, not less than specialists. But I had also to be concerned with parties, which are political institutions with a continuing life of their own, unlike elections (events delimited in time and space). Hence developments in inter-election periods must also be discussed, and it is a nice exercise in political judgement to include only those events which are relevant to the fortunes of the parties. Whether I have succeeded or not is for readers to judge, but at least I tried! Lastly, although research into voting behaviour is still relatively new to Ireland, I have discussed some recent findings in Chapter 8.

At various points in the text and notes I have gratefully acknowledged permission to use copyright material. I wish also to thank those scholars who have helped me in various ways: John Bowman, Basil Chubb, Sydney Elliott, Michael Gallagher, Tom Garvin, Peter Mair, Richard Sinnott, Jack Smith and John Whyte. For any errors of fact or judgement I alone am responsible.

C. O'L.
April 1978

1
Electoral Systems: An Introduction

Although elections have been known since the time of the ancient Greeks, the concept of an electoral *system* is, like much of the institutional furniture of the modern democratic state, of relatively recent origin. Until the nineteenth century, voting methods were regarded as neutral devices to be employed whenever two or more candidates stood for a public office or a seat in a representative assembly. In the British House of Commons, as in other medieval assemblies, elections were originally uncontested. When contests did occur, they followed the same rule as obtained in ecclesiastical elections – the result being determined by a simple majority. The theoretical justification for this was the canonical doctrine of the *maior et sanior pars*, according to which a majority was presumed to be endowed with wisdom superior to that of a minority.[1]

During the four centuries between the first contested election for the House of Commons (in 1450) and the first major extension of the parliamentary franchise in 1832, 'the preponderant tradition in English electoral practice was probably the tradition of uncontested elections'.[2] The same was true of elections to the pre-1800 Irish House of Commons. Even in the nineteenth century, in all but three general elections between one-third and half the constituencies were uncontested and it was not until 1950 that every seat was contested at a Westminster general election.

The Hare System

With the progressive extensions of the franchise in the direction of universal suffrage and the gradual evolution of mass parties, it was perhaps inevitable that the shortcomings of majority voting would be noticed. In 1857, an obscure English barrister named Thomas Hare produced a work entitled *The Machinery of Representation* followed two years later by his better-known *Treatise on the Election of Representatives Parliamentary and Municipal,* in which he drew attention to the vagaries of the traditional method of voting; which, for example, gave both seats in Glasgow to the Liberals and both seats in Liverpool to the Conservatives, although the minority party had substantial support in each city.[3] From the postulate that 'the object of representation was to represent', Hare argued that

1

this would be achieved only when the House of Commons accurately reflected all the shades of political opinion in the country.

Hare's scheme involved three elements:

1. **Multi-member constituencies.** Hare himself envisaged the whole country as a vast constituency in which every voter would have a freedom of choice 'not only of the two or three [under the existing system] but probably of two or three thousand candidates'; but none of his followers would go to this extreme, involving ballot papers of prodigious length and (in all probability) all but the top preferences meaningless. Advocates of the Hare method generally preferred constituencies of not more than ten seats.[4]

2. **The single transferable vote,** marked freely by the voter according to his order of preference between the candidates, irrespective of party. This vote could be transferred if the candidate was eliminated; or, as part of a surplus, if he was elected, provided that a lower preference was numbered on the ballot paper. (If not, it would be non-transferable.)

3. **An electoral quota.** Hare himself would have had the total of votes cast in the United Kingdom divided by the total number of parliamentary seats; but the quota which has generally been associated with the Hare system is the Droop quota,[5] worked out by the formula, Quota = $\frac{\text{Total Valid Poll}}{\text{Seats} + 1} + 1$. Thus, if the total valid poll is 1,000, and the number of seats to be filled is nine, then the quota is 101 votes. (The extra vote is to obviate the possible, but highly unlikely, contingency of ten candidates each getting a quota.)

The Hare system of proportional representation quickly attracted attention in the years before the second Reform Act, when there was much public discussion on the nature and purpose of elections. In *Representative Government* (1861) John Stuart Mill lauded the scheme as 'one of the very greatest improvements yet made in the theory and practice of government', since it involved giving every minority in the nation its fair and equal share of the representation. But Bagehot in a famous passage in his *English Constitution* (1867) poked fun at Mill and Hare: 'The world seems growing young when grave old lawyers and mature philosophers propose a scheme promising so much'.[6] His objection to the Hare system was based on his functional conception of parliament — a body the majority of whose members would support the Cabinet, while the minority would criticise it. The first and most important function would not be fulfilled if the Cabinet's capacity for action were impaired. The formation of a government commanding a parliamentary majority would obviously become more difficult under the Hare scheme, and to Bagehot this was a fundamental drawback.

Mill and Bagehot between them summarised the disputation which has gone on ever since — although in somewhat different terms — as to the purpose of an electoral system; whether it is to provide a 'mirror-image' of the community in the legislature, or a 'collectively effective assembly', capable of forming and sustaining governments.[7]

After the Reform Act of 1867, which established some three-seat constituencies in which voters were given two votes each — a device skilfully exploited by the Liberal organisation (the 'caucus') in Birmingham — the distortions of the majority system became more marked. When the Franchise Bill of 1884 was under consideration, a Liberal MP, Sir John Lubbock, founded the Proportional Representation Society to press the claims of the Hare system on Gladstone. In this he failed, but he succeeded in winning the support of a junior minister, Leonard Courtney (afterwards Lord Courtney of Penwith), who resigned his office and spent the rest of his life crusading for 'electoral justice'.[8] The subsequent history of the PR Society is dealt with below. (For convenience the Hare system is hereinafter referred to as STV.)

The List Systems

In the second half of the nineteenth century, the defects of majority voting also became apparent in Europe, and many schemes of proportional representation were devised. As in England, the theoretical basis of such schemes was individualistic liberalism with its twin requirements of individual participation in political decisions and the need to control governments.[9] In the European context de Tocqueville served as a counterpart to Mill. The first European scheme of PR was elaborated by Victor Considerant for elections in the canton of Geneva in 1846 and possibly the best-known was invented by Victor d'Hondt, a Professor at Ghent university.[10]

All these schemes involved voting primarily for party lists — hence the generic name, **List** systems — but there were many varieties ranging from the completely rigid list (as in the Weimar Republic, 1919-33), where the individual voter was allowed only to mark an 'X' beside the list of a particular party, and the sequence of candidates to be elected followed the order established by the party headquarters, to the completely free list (as in Italy since 1946), where the voter is allowed to express as many preferences as there are candidates on the list. In the first of these cases the voter votes for a party, not a candidate; in the second he is allowed freedom of choice within his chosen party list; in none of the List systems is the voter allowed to crossvote between parties, as in STV, which may be said to maximise the voter's freedom of choice.

Belgium was the first country to adopt a List form of PR for elections to its Chamber of Deputies, in 1899; Finland followed in 1906; Sweden in 1907, and by 1920 every European democracy, except Great Britain and France, had adopted a proportional electoral system.[11]

The Second Ballot

The German Empire between 1870 and 1913 for Reichstag elections, the Third French Republic from 1889 to 1940 for elections to the Chambers of Deputies, and the Fifth French Republic from 1958 for elections to the National Assembly, used a second ballot some weeks after the first election in single-seat constituencies where no candidate had secured a clear majority of the votes. In the second ballot a simple plurality sufficed. The second ballot is generally regarded as being closer to the majority than the proportional systems.[12]

The Alternative Vote

Essentially this is the same as STV, but in single-member constituencies. It is used for elections to the federal House of Representatives and also to some state legislatures in Australia. Although it was incorporated in numerous private members' bills for the British House of Commons, it has never in fact been used for Westminster elections except for those to the one-seat university constituencies of London, Wales and Belfast before the abolition of university representation in 1950.[13]

In Australia this electoral system is known as the **Preferential** vote, which is probably the more accurate description since originally the concept of the alternative vote meant that the voter was limited to *one* choice in the event of his first preference failing to secure election. However, that system has not been tried anywhere for political elections.

Psephologists agree that the alternative vote lies half way between STV and majority voting.[14]

The First-Past-The-Post System

This, the single non-transferable vote in single member constituencies, is the traditional method of voting which was everywhere accepted until the nineteenth century. It is still used for British parliamentary and local elections; in the United States for federal, state and local elections; and in Canada, New Zealand and South Africa. In Britain, apart from the Liberals — and more recently the Scottish and Welsh Nationalists — no political party has campaigned for a change in the electoral system.[15] (In fact the only recent change in United Kingdom elections was the prescription of STV for elections to the Northern Ireland Assembly in 1973 and the Northern Ireland Constitutional Convention in 1975.)[16]

2
Ireland Before 1918: the Road to PR

The PR Society probably reached its peak in the first two decades of the twentieth century. Though private members' bills to introduce STV in Britain met with the same fate as women's suffrage bills, the Society was successful in having STV adopted for elections to the Tasmanian Legislature (1907) and the South African Senate (1909).[1] In 1908 the Society secured the services of a full-time secretary, John H. Humphreys, a very able and tireless publicist, who until his death in 1946 poured out a stream of books and articles reaching into all parts of the British Commonwealth.[2] In 1910 a Royal Commission on Electoral Systems was set up which heard a very strong case for STV from the PR Society. The Commissioners' report was not even debated[3]; but the Speaker's Conference on Electoral Reform (1917) — the first of many — unanimously recommended the introduction of STV. However, as a result of tactical manoeuvrings during the debates on the Representation of the People Bill, 1918, both STV and the Alternative Vote were railroaded out of the bill, and the only concession was the application of STV to university constituencies in the United Kingdom.[4]

Ireland, however, presented a more fruitful field for the advocates of PR. By 1911 the Ulster problem, visible since 1886, was assuming crisis proportions. With the abolition of the Lords' veto by the Parliament Act and the virtual certainty that the third Irish Home Rule Bill would pass into law, the Ulster Unionists, under the determined leadership of Sir Edward Carson, seemed likely to set up a rebellious provisional government rather than submit to the jurisdiction of an all-Ireland parliament.[5] The southern Unionists, a small but highly influential minority, had also to be considered. At this point (January 1911) the PR Society suggested a way out of the impasse. Lord Courtney, then president of the Society, wrote to the veteran Parnellite, Thomas Sexton (who had given up his seat in 1895), advocating a scheme of three- and five-seat constituencies as a solvent of minority fears.[6]

Sexton invited Courtney to Dublin to give a public lecture on STV. Following that lecture in the Antient Concert Rooms (20 April 1911) the Proportional Representation Society of Ireland was formed. Its members included Lord MacDonnell, former Under-Secretary for Ireland; James

5

Creed Meredith KC, author of the first book on PR to be published in Ireland,[7] and later a Supreme Court justice of the Irish Free State; and most significant of all, Arthur Griffith, founder of Sinn Féin, who wrote approvingly of STV: 'Proportional Representation secures that minorities shall be represented in proportion to their strength. It is the one just system of election under democratic government.'[8]

Thus the leader of the new nationalist movement was convinced that PR, by producing seemingly automatic represention for minorities in the proposed Irish legislature, would provide a reasonable protection against the 'tyranny of the majority'. Another important supporter of the idea of PR − though he never joined the Society − was the labour leader James Connolly, soon to enter the pantheon of Irish heroes in Easter week, 1916.

When introduced, the Irish Home Rule Bill of 1912 contained no provision for PR; during the debates, however, amendments were carried adopting STV for elections in constituencies returning three or more members to the new Irish House of Commons—altogether thirty-one seats out of 164—and, after an experimental period of five years, for all the seats in the Senate. The PR Society pressed the Asquith government for further concessions, but only for tactical reasons; they had already secured far more than had seemed possible even two years before.[9]

The outbreak of war in August 1914 and the immediate deferment of the Home Rule Act meant that the new system was never put into operation. It also led to the decline of the PR Society of Ireland, although the Ulster branch survived into the 1920s. It is worth noting, however, that during the debates on the 1912 bill only the Ulster Unionists expressed opposition to STV, on the ground that it was 'un-British'; neither the Irish Parliamentary Party, which still represented the vast majority of the Irish electorate outside Ulster, nor the more militant nationalists of Griffith's following, nor the southern Unionists, raised any objection. Indeed, for many younger people interested in politics the attractiveness of PR went beyond its utility as a device to secure adequate representation for minorities. Forty-five years later, Mrs Nora Connolly-O'Brien, daughter of James Connolly, said in the Irish Senate (5 February 1959): 'I found those principles [of PR] so entwined with the fundamental principles of Labour and Irish Republicanism that I find it difficult to disentangle them and I can no more readily forgo one than the other'.[10]

3
The General Elections of 1918 and 1921

It was again as a device for ensuring minority representation that STV was next heard of in Ireland, in the Sligo Corporation Bill of 1918. This was a private bill, promoted by Thomas Scanlon, Nationalist MP for Sligo County, which aimed to increase the rating powers of the corporation in this very small borough in the west of Ireland, and also to encourage the local Protestant minority to play a more active part in the affairs of the borough. The bill, prescribing STV for future borough council elections in Sligo, passed into law without opposition or debate (July 1918).[1] It was the first successful bill prescribing STV for any part of the United Kingdom.

The elections for the new corporation in Sligo took place one month after the Westminster general election (December 1918). The latter was held with a vast new electorate enfranchised by the Representation of the People Act 1918 (which prescribed universal suffrage for men over twenty-one and women over thirty). In the whole of Ireland the number on the register shot up from 701,475 to 1,936,673. Allowing for natural wastage and war casualties it has been estimated that two out of every three on the register were due to vote for the first time.[2] The result was an unqualified triumph for Sinn Féin. That movement, originally aiming at a dual monarchy, had been reorganised in October 1917 with an unequi- vocal commitment to an Irish Republic, under the presidency of Eamon de Valera, the senior surviving commandant of the Easter Rising. That revolutionary nationalism was replacing the constitutional variety was evident in the results of by-elections held between the beginning of 1917 and the general election; Sinn Féin candidates (including Arthur Griffith, Eamon de Valera and William Thomas Cosgrave) captured seven seats traditionally held by the Irish Parliamentary Party.[3] At the dissolution the Irish representation was sixty-eight Nationalists, ten Independent Nation- alists, eighteen Unionists and seven Sinn Féin. In the general election Sinn Féin carried seventy-three seats, the Unionists went up to twenty-six and the Nationalists were reduced to six seats. All the Unionists (except two members for Trinity College, Dublin) and five of the six Nationalists were returned for Ulster constituencies.

The landslide was not quite so impressive as it appeared on the surface— and not as overwhelming as the electoral victory of Parnell in 1886. The

7

turnout was only sixty-nine per cent and in the contested constituencies only forty-seven per cent of the votes were cast for Sinn Féin. Although in twenty-six constituencies the party candidates were unopposed, contemporary allegations were made that potential opponents were intimidated.[4] To quote F. S. L. Lyons, 'It was . . . a bitter and ugly election, with no holds barred on either side.'[5] Taking electors in uncontested constituencies together with abstentions, 55 per cent of the electorate in what later became the Irish Free State did not vote.[5a]

The results of the Sligo election under STV presented a very different picture. There the Ratepayers' Association (consisting largely of Protestants) headed the poll and Sinn Féin came only second. This result was hailed as a triumph by the PR Society which had sent Mr Humphreys to Sligo to explain the intricacies of STV before the election.[6] It was also lauded by Dublin newspapers of all shades of opinion. The *Freeman's Journal* (18 Jan. 1919) said that STV had produced 'fair representation' and the *Irish Independent* (20 Jan.) averred that it had given Sligo 'a model Council' and that there was no reason why it should not be equally successful in Dublin and other cities and towns in Ireland: these favourable comments from two organs in the Nationalist tradition were reinforced by the pro-Unionist *Irish Times,* which asserted that PR was 'the *magna charta* of political and municipal minorities' (18 Jan.).

But more stirring events were at hand to claim popular attention. On 21 January 1919 the Sinn Féin representatives took the first step towards their separatist goal by constituting themselves as an all-Ireland parliament in Dublin, although no Unionist attended their deliberations. This assembly, known to history as the first Dáil, set up a Cabinet of which de Valera was president, and Griffith a member.[7] Although the British government at once proscribed the Dáil and arrested several of its members, it continued to meet secretly and to solicit aid and recognition from abroad, especially from the United States and the Versailles congress. As is well known, the meeting of the first Dáil inaugurated a two-and-a-half year period of military repression and guerrilla insurgency (the War of Independence.)

It was against this turbulent background in the last years of British rule that further electoral experiments were made. Early in 1919, the Lloyd George government introduced a bill prescribing STV for elections to local authorities throughout Ireland. During the debates on the bill the Attorney General for Ireland (A. W. Samuels KC) frankly admitted that the government hoped thereby to blunt the edge of Sinn Féin success in the three southern provinces, and likewise to secure Nationalist representation in Ulster.[8] When the local elections were held (January 1920) the results fulfilled the government's intentions in the North (where Derry City and Counties Tyrone and Fermanagh returned Nationalist-controlled councils, while Belfast Corporation contained for the first time several significant minority groups[9]), but not in the south, where Sinn Féin had a clean sweep of all the local authorities – in fact most elections were uncontested. By then the south of Ireland was convulsed by the guerrilla war between the (original) Irish Republican Army, commanded by Michael Collins, and the Auxiliaries and 'Black and Tans'.

Next, the Lloyd George coalition set to work to produce a scheme 'for the better government of Ireland', which eventually became the Government of Ireland Act, 1920. This act established two Irish political systems —governments and parliaments in Dublin and Belfast with identical powers and limitations for the twenty-six and six counties respectively, with a Council of Ireland to consult on matters of common interest.[10] Both parliaments were to be bicameral, the popular House in each case being elected by STV. When the bill was being debated at Westminster the Ulster Unionists (now led by Sir James Craig, since Carson had become a Lord of Appeal) showed no great enthusiasm for the new provincial institutions, but were prepared to accept them in preference to an all-Ireland political system. Their aversion to the 'un-British' STV was not mitigated by the results of the local elections described above.

Elections for the two parliaments took place in May 1921. Neither remotely resembled a typical PR election, which was not surprising in view of the disturbed state of the country. In the parliament of Northern Ireland the Unionists won forty out of fifty-two seats, a higher total than they were ever to win under the first-past-the-post system, to which they reverted in 1929. The remaining seats were divided (as a result of a pre-election agreement) between the old Nationalist Party, led by Joseph Devlin, and Sinn Féin, each winning six seats. Neither the Nationalist nor the Sinn Féin members (including de Valera, Griffith and Collins) took their seats.[11]

The election to the parliament of 'southern Ireland' was even more remarkable. While all the constituencies in Northern Ireland were contested, all the constituencies in the south were uncontested, and this election remains the only one in a western democracy with this feature. Before the election John Dillon, the last leader of the Irish Parliamentary Party, stated that the repressive policy of the British government had made it practically impossible for a nationalist Irishman to fight Sinn Féin.[12] So Sinn Féin won 124 out of the 128 seats, the remainder going to four Independents from Trinity College, Dublin.[13]

The elections of May 1921 clearly demonstrated the impossibility on any democratic hypothesis of British rule continuing in the twenty-six counties; and, on the other hand, the desire of some two-thirds of the electorate of the six counties to remain in the United Kingdom. The parliament of southern Ireland was stillborn, the Sinn Féin members continuing to meet separately under the appellation, the Second Dáil. Within two months of the election a truce was arranged between the British forces in the south and the Irish Republican Army, and in October 1921 six delegates from the Second Dáil, under the leadership of Arthur Griffith, went to London to negotiate a settlement with the British government.[14]

The history of the Anglo-Irish settlement of 1921 and the birth pangs of the new state amid civil war do not concern us here. It will suffice to set the chronological pattern:

1. On 6 December 1921 the Irish delegates signed a treaty with six representatives of the British government, including the Prime Minister, Lloyd George, which gave the twenty-six counties (to be known as the Irish Free State) dominion status, while reserving certain naval facilities to the British government. The treaty formally applied to the whole of Ireland, but the parliament of Northern Ireland was given the right to opt out within a period of six months. This was done in May 1922 and Northern Ireland continued with the same degree of autonomy as under the Government of Ireland Act.

2. Publication of the terms of the agreement caused an immediate split in the Sinn Féin party. Almost half the Dáil deputies (including two members of the Dáil Cabinet, Cathal Brugha and Austin Stack, as well as President de Valera) argued for its rejection, on the ground that to accept the trappings of dominion status—the oath of allegiance to the King and the office of Governor General—would be to compromise their Republican pledges. (On the other hand, the continuance of a separate regime for Northern Ireland was reluctantly conceded.) The others favoured accepting the Treaty as a stepping stone to further constitutional advancement; and, more realistically, as the best settlement that could be obtained at that time. The months of December 1921 and January 1922 were consumed in acrimonious debate and eventually the Dáil passed the Treaty by the narrow margin of sixty-four votes to fifty-seven.[15]

3. De Valera at once resigned his office and the Dáil elected Griffith to succeed him, not as 'President of the Republic' (the title de Valera had held since August 1921) but as 'President of Dáil Éireann' (the title he had held from April 1919). Although Griffith nominated a Cabinet from among the pro-Treaty deputies, by a curious duplication of function a provisional government was also set up under the chairmanship of Michael Collins, the commander-in-chief of the revolutionary army, to arrange for the transfer of powers from the British administration.[16]

4. In the early months of 1922 de Valera and his followers agitated throughout the country against implementation of the Treaty. This posed an additional problem for the Provisional Government. By the Treaty they were obliged to secure popular approval before implementation, but the prospect of an election campaign free of intimidation seemed extremely remote. As a *faute de mieux* Collins made an agreement with de Valera in May 1922 to present to the voters a joint panel of candidates, in the same proportions of Treatyites and anti-Treatyites as in the existing Dáil. This electoral pact has been criticised as 'a direct denial of a primary principle of representative democracy'.[17] Its clear meaning was that the people would not be given an opportunity of expressing an opinion on the most important issue an Irish electorate had ever faced—the constitutional

future of the country. It is true that one clause of the Pact permitted other candidatures, but if that had not happened (at Collins' insistence) the election would not have been in any sense free. It might be wondered how de Valera could have expected to prevent other parties and Independents from standing in spite of the Pact; but in 1918 many and in 1921 all the seats had been uncontested; so it was not entirely unrealistic to hope that at least the facade of the unanimity that had prevailed during the previous four years might have been preserved.[18] De Valera also wished to forestall an open conflict between the two wings of Sinn Féin, which seemed inevitable as time went on.

4

The 'Pact Election' of 1922 and the Constitution of the Irish Free State

I

The 'Pact Election' was held under conditions of considerable disturbance (June 1922).[1] In addition to the agreed panel of Sinn Féin candidates (sixty-five pro-Treaty and fifty-nine anti-Treaty), fifty-two other candidates were nominated (eighteen Labour, thirteen Farmers and twenty-one Independents). The constituencies were the same as had been drawn up by the Government of Ireland Act and used for the election of 1921 — two 8-seat, one 7-seat, two 6-seat, four 5-seat, sixteen 4-seat, and three 3-seat constituencies. When the high degree of proportionality in the constituency arrangements is taken into account the large number of unopposed returns (thirty-eight out of 128 seats) furnishes proof that conditions were still far from normal. However, the contested constituencies produced the following result:

Treatyites	41
Anti-Treatyites	19
Labour	17
Farmers	7
Independents	6

The uncontested areas returned seventeen Treatyites, seventeen anti-Treatyites and four Independents.

After the election the Labour, Farmer and Independent deputies declared their support for the Treaty, which meant that the anti-Treatyites could not muster more than thirty-six out of 128 deputies. Bitterly protesting that they had been tricked by evasions of the electoral pact, de Valera's followers refused to take their seats in the Third Dáil.[2]

In the same month civil war broke out between the two factions and continued in a desultory manner until April 1923. The number of casualties was small—the supply of arms on the government side assured its ultimate success—but they included two ministers of the First and Second Dáil Cabinets, Michael Collins (commander-in-chief of the government forces) and Cathal Brugha, who rejected the Treaty. The bitterness gener-

12

ated by the conflict made it psychologically impossible for the main participants on both sides ever again to cooperate politically, as they had during the years of the War of Independence.[3]

II

While the civil war was in progress the Third Dáil set about providing the Irish Free State with a constitution. The death of Arthur Griffith in August 1922 and the assassination of Michael Collins three weeks later removed the reason, if there ever had been one, for two executives; and at the first meeting of the Dáil, in September, the deputies elected W. T. Cosgrave, Minister for Local Government, as 'President of the Dáil',[4] and he nominated a Cabinet which was approved by the Dáil and also constituted the Provisional Government.

In January 1922 the Provisional Government had set up a special committee to draft a new constitution. The Constitutional Committee (a well-balanced combination of lawyers, academics and civil servants) could not agree on a single draft, so several were presented. (Despite their obvious intrinsic interest the Provisional Government did not publish the drafts, except the one which they themselves subsequently approved.)[5] That constitution was published on 16 June 1922, the day of the Pact Election, and thus it could not be claimed that the electorate were presented with an opportunity to give a reasoned judgment on its contents.

The draft constitution[6] provided in general for a British-style system: a bicameral legislature, Dáil and Seanad (Senate), and Cabinet government with the executive responsible to the lower house. But there were some provisions ensuring the supremacy of the Dáil over both Senate and government. The head of the government, styled President of the Executive Council, was not (as is customary in parliamentary political systems) appointed by the Head of State (in this case, the Governor General, acting for the King), but was to be elected by the Dáil, and each of his ministers had to be approved by the Dáil. The Executive Council, if defeated, could not precipitate a dissolution. The constitution also provided for 'extern' ministers, who would not be members of the Executive Council but would be responsible directly to the Dáil.[7]

As to the electoral system, the Constitution prescribed full adult suffrage —six years before Great Britain—and directed that the 153 deputies of the Dáil be elected 'upon the principles of Proportional Representation' (Art. 26). The same article fixed the ratio of members to population at not less than one for every 30,000 people, nor more than one for every 20,000. The drawing-up of constituencies and the nature of the voting methods were to be settled by ordinary law. Thus the Constitution did not specify the mode of PR to be adopted; but it prescribed that the constituencies be revised every ten years to take account of population changes.[8]

Apart from PR, the new political system strongly resembled the British

13

one, although with the written Constitution greater precision could be attained in defining the powers of the public authorities. Nevertheless, the Constitutional Committee, as the most distinguished member, Chief Justice Kennedy, later testified, did not consider itself under any obligation to follow the British model.[9] Not only were the checks on the executive and the extern ministers important deviations, but the prevailing attitude to political parties (not mentioned in the Constitution) was that they were at best necessary evils, and one of the rejected drafts (prepared by Professor Alfred O'Rahilly of University College, Cork) envisaged the evolution of a non-party system.[10]

There are three main reasons that may be assigned for the inclusion of PR in the Free State Constitution:

1. In Europe after the First World War, PR was considered as a necessary concomitant of democracy. It was incorporated into the constitutions of all the new states established in 1918-19, almost without discussion. The Constitutional Committee, which took the trouble to prepare a digest of some eighty existing constitutions, was keenly aware of this trend.[11]

2. The campaign which had been waged by the PR Society—and its Irish branch—since 1911 had been well publicised. From 1919 onwards the literature of the Society was full of glowing tributes to the effectiveness of the Sligo election, and the local government elections in Ulster in 1920.[12] Conversely there was no pressure group to advocate the retention of the first-past-the-post system.

3. Most important of all, Arthur Griffith had given to two distinguished southern Unionists, on 6 December 1921 (the day of the signing of the Treaty), a guarantee of due representation for southern Unionists in the Senate and the adoption of STV for elections to the Dáil. These undertakings were confirmed in a letter from Griffith to Lloyd George.[13] (Griffith's early interest in PR has been mentioned above, and during the Treaty negotiations he is reported to have said that he was 'the first to preach it in Ireland'.)[14]

Thus the introduction of PR into the Free State Constitution was due not only to current practice in European democracies and to the efforts of a well-organised pressure group nearer home, but also to the necessity for satisfying the fears and susceptibilities of a powerful minority, the southern Protestants, whose influence at the upper levels of business and the professions, not to speak of the landowning class which they had always dominated, was out of all proportion to their numbers—about 9 per cent of the population.

That the minority was satisfied with the promise of PR was itself the consequence of the propaganda for 'electoral justice'. But unless the southern Unionists intended to form a new political party and try their luck at the polls, the new system could not help them. As we shall see, the Protestant (and ex-Unionist) element in the early Dáils became absorbed by the main parties—a result which could have been equally well achieved under majority voting.

But it was what STV was believed *capable* of achieving that mattered in 1922. Griffith, who was particularly anxious to conciliate the Protestant-Unionist population, believed that it would guarantee them a certain voice in the legislature. The same view was shared by the organ of Protestant opinion, the *Irish Times,* which had lauded the Sligo experiment and jubilantly wrote after the local election of 1920 that 'the system of proportional representation has come to stay'.[15]

The Provisional Government had the additional reason that the use of the same system as that of the partitioned Six Counties could help towards reunification. They could not have foreseen the debacle of the Boundary Commission three years later, nor that four years afterwards the Northern Ireland government would revert to majority voting.[16]

During the months of September and October 1922 the Third Dáil acted as a constituent assembly, examining in detail the provisions of the draft constitution. The electoral provisions caused little discussion. The speeches revealed a complete ignorance of the List systems—in spite of Justice Meredith's book—and it soon became plain that the constitutional directive was to be interpreted as prescribing STV, the only form of PR of which Ireland had had any experience.[17]

The Constitution was promulgated by decree on 25 October 1922, and came into effect on 6 December 1922, the first anniversary of the Treaty. Cosgrave was elected the first President of the Executive Council and nominated a cabinet of six ministers and three extern ministers. The monarchical provisions of the Constitution which were mandatory under the Treaty—the Governor General representing the King and the oath of allegiance to be taken by all members of the Oireachtas (parliament)—were abhorrent to the Republicans. They also disliked the Senate, half of which was filled by ex-Unionists, nominated by Cosgrave, in fulfilment of Griffith's promise. The Cosgrave government came to dislike some of the provisions of their own Constitution, notably those for an initiative or referendum on constitutional amendments; but they were able to avail themselves of a provision whereby the Constitution during the first eight years of its existence might be amended by ordinary law to get rid of these encumbrances.[18]

The law determining the 'mode and place of exercising this right' (of universal suffrage) was the Electoral Act, 1923, which laid down the detailed rules for operating STV, and divided up the Irish Free State into thirty constituencies returning between three and nine deputies each (Galway county was the solitary nine-seat constituency), totalling 153, or an average of 5.1 deputies per constituency. This compares with a total of twenty-eight constituencies, 128 deputies, and an average of 4.6 deputies per constituency under the Government of Ireland Act. There were two university constituencies, the graduates of Dublin University (Trinity College, Dublin) and the National University of Ireland each electing three deputies—another legacy of the British system, since this form of specialised representation has never been known outside Great Britain and some of its dependencies.[19]

The Dáil debates on the Electoral Bill were as unoriginal as those on the electoral provisions of the Constitution. There was no question of an alternative form of PR, nor a reversion to the first-past-the-post system. As the *Irish Times* predicted, PR had come to stay, and if the PR Society could not claim all the credit it was certainly entitled to a large share.

5

The Multi-Party System, 1923-57

In considering Irish electoral history from the establishment of the Irish Free State to the present day two main phases may be discerned: between 1923 and 1957 there was a multi-party system, and from 1961 to the present a two-and-a-half party system. The reasons for adopting this model, rather than more elaborate models proposed by other scholars, are given in Chapter 8.[1]

1923-37

The general election for the Fourth Dáil, held in August 1923, was not only the first under the new Constitution and electoral law but it was the first in Ireland, since that of December 1910, to be held in what approximated to normal political conditions. Admittedly the government persisted in repressive policies against the anti-Treatyites even though the civil war had ended in May with their decisive defeat. But, as is shown below, this did not significantly affect their electoral performance.[2]

The election of 1923 was the first in Irish history in which every territorial constituency was contested—the exact opposite of that of 1921. Perhaps encouraged by the claims that had been made for STV and by the large-scale constituencies, 375 candidates stood for the 153 seats—apart from June 1927 that total was not exceeded until 1948—and the number of competing groups was nineteen! Four, however, deserve special mention.

(a) *Cumann na nGaedheal.* In January 1923 a convention of pro-Treaty deputies (hitherto variously described as the 'Government Party', the 'Ministry Party'[3] or the 'Treaty Party') agreed to organise themselves into a new party, which was formally launched in April 1923, and took the name Cumann na nGaedheal (League of the Irish), which had been used by an early Sinn Féin group, under the leadership of President Cosgrave. The very circumstances of its foundation show an absence of policy or class interest. By avoiding any criterion for membership apart from acceptance of the Treaty and the new Constitution, Cosgrave hoped to bring into his party 'the best elements of the country, irrespective of class or creed'.[4] To pursue such an aim in the unstable conditions of the time displays an imperfect understanding of the nature of a political party, and there is evidence that several of Cosgrave's ministers were not really 'party-minded'.

17

(Before long there developed a dispute over free trade and protection on which members of the government held violently conflicting views.[5])

The yardstick of the Treaty, peace and ordered government, was enough for the new party to win over the propertied classes—the large farmers and the upper levels in commerce, industry and the professions, who had looked askance at Sinn Féin between 1918 and 1922. Nevertheless, for a governing party Cumann na nGaedheal made a poor showing in the 1923 election, winning a mere 39 per cent of the votes and sixty-three seats—not much more than a third of the Dáil.

(b) *Sinn Féin.* After the ending of the civil war the anti-Treatyites had to decide whether to contest the general election which was expected after the passing of the Electoral Act.[6] Although Sinn Féin had been split down the middle over the Treaty issue, its headquarters closed down and its branches disbanded, de Valera decided to reorganise the Republicans to fight the election under the old name Sinn Féin (the third party of that name)—which drew protests from some of the Treatyites. The Sinn Féin electoral programme was simply outright refusal to accept the Free State, and they were committed to boycotting the Dáil, if elected. In spite of harassment by the government (over 12,000 Republicans were in jail, including de Valera, who was arrested during the election campaign), the loss of prestige consequent on their civil war defeat, and their sterile abstentionist policy, Sinn Féin nominated eighty-five candidates and won 27.4 per cent of the total vote and forty-four seats out of 153.

Sinn Féin was easily the leading opposition party, although their adherence to the abstentionist policy made things a good deal easier for the government, which was able to continue on a single-party basis. It has been estimated that de Valera kept the support of the small farmers, shopkeepers and sections of the working class who had five and six years before provided the nucleus of Sinn Féin support.[7] The personal prestige of de Valera, still styled 'President of the Republic', and the emotive appeal of doctrinaire nationalism also worked in favour of Sinn Féin. On its showing in 1923, the Republican Party was, even at the lowest ebb in its fortunes, a force to be reckoned with, and any hopes the Cosgrave government might have entertained of its electoral annihilation were disappointed.

(c) *Labour.* This was the oldest party.[8] In 1912 the Irish Trade Union Congress (which had been in existence since 1894) decided after the English example to found a political wing, the Irish Labour Party, which gradually extended throughout the country. Its founding fathers were James Larkin (who had also founded the largest Irish union, the Irish Transport and General Workers' Union, in 1909) and his chief associate, James Connolly, who took over when Larkin left for the United States in 1914. Both Larkin and Connolly were avowed revolutionary socialists.

Connolly and a section of the Labour movement in Dublin played an active part in the Easter Rising, but the party as such was not officially involved.[9] Nevertheless the Rising had a traumatic effect on Labour in

18

Dublin; its leader was executed, its headquarters destroyed and several members imprisoned and deported. In 1917 Thomas Johnson, a moderate, English-born socialist, succeeded Connolly as leader of the party; his aim was to keep the party (which still had branches in Ulster) intact by concentrating on social and economic issues.[10] But in the perfervid atmosphere of 1917-18 this was impossible; the Labour Party in the south became thoroughly Republican in outlook, and the northern branches gradually went their own way, eventually becoming the Northern Ireland Labour Party in 1923.[11]

When the election of 1918 drew near, the Labour Party at first resolved to enter the lists as an independent party, but under pressure from Sinn Féin decided to stand aside and leave a clear field to the latter. So in 'the most momentous election of twentieth-century Ireland' the Labour Party was unrepresented,[12] and there was no Labour voice in the First Dáil. In the vivid words of Peadar O'Donnell, Labour 'confused the prompter's stool with a place on the stage'.[13] A similar policy was followed in 1921—except by Richard Corish (Labour Mayor of Wexford) who defied official party policy and stood as a Sinn Féin candidate in Wexford.[14] Labour did not come into its own until the Pact Election, when it put up eighteen candidates, of whom seventeen were successful, including Johnson, the leader, and several who were to have long political careers—Corish, William Davin, James Everett and Daniel Morrissey. Comparisons with later elections are difficult, since several constituencies were uncontested; but in the contested constituencies Labour actually fared nearly as well as the anti-Treatyites, with 132,565 votes to 135,309.

In 1923 the Labour Party nominated forty-four candidates and secured nearly the same aggregate vote as in the previous year, but won only fourteen seats out of 153 (compared with seventeen out of 128). It fared worse in Dublin than in Waterford or Wexford! This was partly due to the restricted appeal of the party: it was still very much the political wing of the trade union movement; its members were almost entirely drawn from trade unions and about half of them were union officials.[15] There was no attempt to broaden the appeal or the social composition of the party, as the British Labour Party had so successfully done after 1918. But even though Ireland was still a predominantly agricultural country and the urban proletariat was small, one would have expected Labour to pick up more than one seat in Dublin in 1923. A probable reason for that particularly poor showing was that in April 1923 James Larkin returned, after over eight years in America, a convinced communist, and at once began a feud with his 'gradualist' deputy William O'Brien (who had built up the ITGWU into a union of over 100,000 members). This resulted in Larkin's expulsion from both the union and the party which he had founded, and was to have dire long-term consequences for both.[16]

(d) *Farmers.* This was a purely sectional party, the political wing of the Farmers' Union whose interests it existed to promote.[17] In the Pact Election the Farmers' Party won seven seats, and in 1923, having nominated sixty-five candidates, secured fifteen seats. All the seats were won in rural constituencies, but since the farming community counted for at least half of the total electorate it was plain that many farmers voted Cumann na nGaedheal. The party policies were conservative—free trade and economy in public spending; and it was strongly in support of the Treaty.

In the Fourth Dáil the Farmers generally supported the government and so Labour became the official opposition.

Of the minor groups (Business, Ratepayers, Town Tenants, etc.) all failed to secure representation except two 'Business' candidates in Dublin. But altogether minor groups and Independents secured nearly 11 per cent of the votes, and 9 per cent of the seats, a result more characteristic of PR than majority-type elections.

The main parties securing representation in 1923 do not fall into the stock categories beloved of political sociologists. Only the Farmers were purely an interest group, and none of the other three was strictly a class party. The bulk of the deputies belonged to the two parties which owed their existence to the split in the post-1918 revolutionary nationalist movement.

On the other hand the nature of the revolutionary movement of itself predisposed towards schism.[18] The second Sinn Féin party had been an uneasy coalition between militants who were 'politicians by accident' (de Valera's own description), and people reared in the liberal democratic tradition of the Irish Parliamentary Party, who had temporarily resorted to violence but were not enamoured of it; Cosgrave's deputy, Kevin O'Higgins, and the academics from University College, Dublin, were plainly in this category.[19] A study of the Treaty debates shows the profound division between the two approaches, and it is reasonable to speculate that if the Treaty issue had not arisen some other issue would have been found to force these latent differences into the open.[20] The civil war was no accident.

This point cannot be stressed too much, since the revolutionary anti-democratic element, although going underground a few years after 1927, has repeatedly surfaced again to disturb Irish politics. It has deep roots in Irish history which have helped it to survive so long; its characteristic attitude is intolerant, doctrinaire and utterly impervious to argument. The canonisation of the Republic proclaimed in 1916, which the people of ten, twenty or even fifty years later should not dare to repudiate, and the persistent ignoring of majority opinion in Northern Ireland are the most obvious manifestations of this ideological bigotry.[21] But from the civil war Republicans down to the Provisional IRA it has been a powerful, though intermittent, political force.

Thus the Treaty issue, or to put it in a wider context the choice between becoming a full self-governing member of the British Commonwealth and a small isolated republic, gave an extra dimension to the social composition of the two main parties. Broadly speaking, both were middle-class parties, with Cumann na nGaedheal attracting the upper and Sinn Féin the lower middle classes. But they were parliamentary parties before they became mass parties, and they did not develop mass organisations until later.[22]

Another factor making for a two-way cleavage was the rivalry between de Valera and Cosgrave. The personality of de Valera was so outstanding—especially after the deaths of Griffith, Collins and Brugha—that in a country like Ireland, with memories of Parnell and fainter memories of O'Connell,[23] his existence alone would have sufficed to create a movement or a party. As head of the established government Cosgrave was his obvious rival and to many people—it is impossible to say how many, but they must have been far from few—the politics of the Irish Free State must have been regarded as a struggle for power between the two leaders and their supporting groups.

One further question must be considered before we pass from the formative year, 1923: whether the retention of majority voting might have altered significantly the balance of parties. Certainly the assumption that, with the first-past-the-post system, Cumann na nGaedheal would have secured an enormous majority and Sinn Féin would have been annihilated is quite untenable. The first-past-the-post system normally gives a premium of seats to the largest party, but for the premium to be substantial the lead in votes must also be substantial. A poll of less than 40 per cent, such as Cumann na nGaedheal achieved, has never produced a landslide, nor has a party with over 25 per cent of the votes (such as Sinn Féin secured) ever been drastically reduced. In fact, when the gap between the major parties narrows, the results may approximate to proportionality. In the Westminster election of 1923,[24] when the Conservatives secured 38 per cent and the Liberals 29.6 per cent of the votes (a distribution very similar to that of Cumann na nGaedheal and Sinn Féin), the results in seats were 258 and 159 respectively. A fate similar to that of the Liberals, who in 1959 got 6 per cent of the votes and 1 per cent of the seats, has historically been reserved for parties falling below 15 per cent of the national vote.

On the hypothesis of majority voting Cumann na nGaedheal would probably have secured a few more seats but scarcely the extra fourteen needed for an overall majority. Although Labour and Farmers would probably have been drastically reduced, some of the Independents might have been elected—particularly three ex-Unionists with strong local support in Dublin and Donegal.[25]

The overall result of the 1923 election meant that Cumann na nGaedheal was a minority government. Had the followers of de Valera taken their seats, Cosgrave would have been forced into a coalition with the Farmers—as happened in 1927—and even then would have controlled a bare majority of the Dáil. But, as a result of Sinn Féin abstention, he enjoyed a fortuitous majority, and between 1923 and 1927 his policies were characterised by a boldness rarely associated with minority governments.

Two important developments in the party system occurred during the first four years of the Irish Free State.

1. Convinced of the futility of abstentionism, de Valera decided in 1926 to form a political party pledged *inter alia* to removing the obnoxious monarchical elements from the Constitution when it attained power.[26] The issue came to a head at the annual Ard Fheis (policy-making conference) of Sinn Féin in March 1926 when de Valera proposed a resolution allowing the Republican representatives to attend both Irish assemblies, if the requirement of the oath were removed. This was opposed by those in Sinn Féin for whom 'almost four years of abstentionism had elevated the issue to the level of inalterable dogma'[27] and de Valera's motion was defeated by a narrow margin (223 votes to 218). Two days later, on 11 March 1926, de Valera tendered his resignation as president of Sinn Féin (a title he had held for nine years) and two weeks later as 'President of the Republic'. In May 1926 he launched a new party under the poetic name Fianna Fáil (Soldiers of Destiny). Its programme consisted of more than doctrinaire republicanism and the development of the Irish language (already initiated by the Cosgrave government); it also included protection for native industry and economies in the public service. Later, the economic programme was complemented by a welfare programme, more advanced than any non-socialist party offered before Roosevelt's New Deal. De Valera plainly hoped to attract many voters who had opposed him in the past by 'his rare combination of a revolutionary objective with a conservative appeal'.[28]

Of the outgoing Republican deputies twenty-three refused to contemplate entering the Dáil and clung to the name Sinn Féin in stubborn isolation, while twenty-one followed de Valera into what one of the youngest and most able of them, Sean Lemass, quaintly called 'a slightly constitutional party'.[29]

2. During the lifetime of the Fourth Dáil two splinter groups emerged from within the government party. In 1924 nine deputies, led by the Minister for Industry and Commerce, Joseph McGrath, resigned from Cumann na nGaedheal and formed the National Party. The efficient cause was the firm handling by the government of an abortive mutiny within the army, which also led to the resignation of the Minister for Defence, General Richard Mulcahy. When the government refused to reinstate the leaders of the mutiny the National Party resigned their seats *en bloc* and precipitated a mini-general election—nine simultaneous by-elections. The results, however, were disastrous for the new party, all of whose deputies failed to be returned, and the National Party disappeared.[30]

In 1925, the report of the Boundary Commission, which left the territory of Northern Ireland virtually intact, caused great disappointment

22

generally in the Free State. Two Cumann na nGaedheal deputies led by Professor William Magennis (Professor of Metaphysics in University College, Dublin and a deputy for the National University of Ireland) broke away to form a party called Clann Eireann, with a vaguely Republican programme not very unlike that of Fianna Fáil.[31] A more serious threat was posed by another new party—the third to be founded in 1926 — called the National League, led by Captain William Redmond, the son of John Redmond and the only candidate from the Irish Parliamentary Party to win a seat in the south in 1918. Redmond's appeal was to former supporters of his father's party who had not already come round to supporting Cumann na nGaedheal; to the thousands of British ex-servicemen who had returned to Ireland in the years after the war, and to various disaffected sectional interests, especially the licensed vintners who had been outraged by restrictive legislation introduced by the government.[32]

Lastly, there was the embryonic Irish communist movement. The tiny Communist Party of Ireland, founded in 1921 under the presidency of Roddy Connolly, the youthful son of James Connolly, was dissolved on orders from the Comintern following the return of Larkin from the United States in 1923, and ordered to join Larkin's new organisation, the Irish Worker League. They fondly believed that this would evolve into a mass communist party, but it was essentially a vehicle for Larkin's highly individualistic brand of politics.[33]

This meant that eight parties already represented in the Dáil (including Sinn Féin and two Independent Republicans) and other Independents contested the election of June 1927. This time the electoral system produced what might be called a typical PR result. While the government party lost sixteen seats and was reduced to a mere 30 per cent of the Dáil, Fianna Fáil secured the same number of seats as Sinn Féin in 1923, although its proportion of the vote was slightly lower. Between them the two major parties controlled 59 per cent of the seats—the lowest proportion in any election in our period. The beneficiaries were Labour, the National League, and the dissident Republicans. Clann Éireann secured a derisory vote and their two outgoing members were defeated. The National League put up thirty candidates and won eight seats.[34]

The election result for the first time raised the question of a coalition, since Fianna Fáil was determined to participate in the Dáil. Cumann na nGaedheal, even with support from Farmers and Independents, was still in a minority, and the two-month life of this shortest Dáil was spent in manoeuvring for position by the various groups. Eventually an arrangement between Fianna Fáil, Labour and the National League to bring down the government was foiled by the singular Jinks Affair, and the government, having won a vote of confidence on the casting vote of the Ceann Comhairle (Speaker) of the Dáil, declared another election.[35] This election again simplified the party system. The minor parties all lost, the National League being virtually and the Independent Republicans actually

23

eliminated—Sinn Féin did not even contest the election. On the other hand, Larkin's Irish Worker League, with a revolutionary socialist programme, nominated three candidates in Dublin, including Larkin himself, who was elected for the first time. (The intervention of his son, James Larkin Junior, cost Thomas Johnson, the Labour leader, his seat.) The election was generally disastrous for Labour, which lost nine of its twenty-two seats, while the two main parties made considerable gains.[36]

Since Cumann na nGaedheal now held a slender lead of four seats over Fianna Fáil, Cosgrave was forced into a formal coalition with the Farmers —which had in fact been proposed before the June election. The recovery of the major parties was probably helped by three factors:

(a) The assassination of Vice-President Kevin O'Higgins by unknown, armed men in July 1927 revived fears of revolutionary violence lulled by the peaceful developments of the previous four years, and this worked to the government's advantage.

(b) The jockeying for power by the minor groups during the short life of the Dáil was skilfully spotlighted in the election propaganda of Cumann na nGaedheal. An advertisement appearing on the eve of the (June) election *had* warned the electorate that there were three choices: a de Valera single-party government, a Cosgrave single-party government and a coalition. Having instanced what might be expected from the first two, the advertisement specified the following qualities of coalitions:

This is what you are voting for if you give your first vote to Independents, Farmers or Labour:

It means:

1. Bargaining for place and power between irresponsible Minority groups.
2. A weak Government with no stated policy.
3. Frequent changes of Government.
4. Consequent depression in Trade and Industry.
5. No progress, but stability, security and credit in constant danger.[37]

No contemporary evidence was cited in support of these propositions— although the government might have mentioned the political conditions then existing in the Weimar Republic, or in Italy before 1922. Cumann na nGaedheal clearly went on record as being opposed to coalitions. But if it had not been able to dissolve the Dáil, it would have been forced into one on much more unfavourable terms than in the following September. In 1958 Ernest Blythe, who succeeded Kevin O'Higgins as Vice-President of the Executive Council, revealed that it was John A. Costello, then Attorney General, who advised the Executive Council that the Constitution did not prevent it from dissolving the Dáil without its consent.[38]

(c) The new comprehensive programme of Fianna Fáil, and the fact that its deputies had taken their seats after the June election helped to make them respectable in the eyes of the better-off voters.

At any rate from 1927 to 1932 the Cosgrave government was to all appearances a 'lame duck' administration, with the most meagre of Dáil majorities and the knowledge from by-election results that their ex-revolutionary rivals were making the pendulum swing in their favour.[39] On one occasion in 1930 Cosgrave was defeated in the Dáil and resigned, but he resumed office since de Valera was unwilling to form either a minority government or a coalition. Another card in de Valera's hand was the organisational one. His party quickly built up a mass organisation based on the parish club (or cumann) with constituency executives, a national executive and an annual policy-making conference (the Ard Fheis).[40] The Cumann na nGaedheal Party had the same interlocking system from the level of the constituency association upwards, but was lamentably deficient in local associations. It relied far too much on an elite in the large towns. Fianna Fáil, on the other hand, established a cumann in almost every parish to canalise the energies of its followers and provide a breeding ground for party talent. The method was similar to that employed by Sinn Féin before 1918 but the Fianna Fáil cumainn were a good deal more extensive than the Sinn Féin clubs. Loyalty to the leadership became such a cardinal principle in Fianna Fáil thinking that no danger has ever arisen of local cumainn forming splinter groups or seeking to determine policy, apart from during their annual ventilation of grievances at the Ard Fheis.

Before the first general election of 1927 de Valera (following the example of Parnell in 1880) made a special trip to the United States and raised enough from Irish-American friends and admirers to finance the two campaigns.[41] But from the beginning the usual Fianna Fáil means of fundraising was an annual collection at church doors throughout the country on a particular day.

The organisation of the Labour Party, on paper the same as the others, did not go below the constituency level, except in the cities and larger towns. In the Farmers' Party the few local associations were virtually autonomous and there was no national organisation apart from the Parliamentary Party.

Fianna Fáil party morale was given a further fillip in 1931 with the establishment of the only national daily newspaper in the Free State to be controlled by a political party—the *Irish Press*. Of the other two Dublin dailies, the *Irish Independent* was, as a rule, in favour of the status quo, and the former Unionist organ, the *Irish Times*, was gradually coming round to the support of Cumann na nGaedheal. Both shared in a profound hostility to de Valera. From its inception the *Irish Press* was a purely partisan newspaper giving the maximum amount of coverage to the pronouncements of Fianna Fáil leaders and other news of party interest.

The other parties did not rise above small weekly or monthly papers. It was in one of these, however, the Cumann na nGaedheal weekly *An Realt (The Star)*, that the first wholehearted denunciation of the Irish PR system appeared (10 May, 1930). It is worth quoting at some length:

One of the factors which has delayed normal political development in the Saorstat (Free State) is our bad electoral system. The particular form of Proportional Representation which is in force here is perhaps not so bad as that in force in Germany but that is the best that can be said about it.

Having emphasised that the system was 'thrust upon the country by the British,' the writer went on:

The main objection to Proportional Representation is that it inevitably operates in such a way as to be non-democratic. In this country the fundamental evils of the system have not made themselves fully apparent yet, because complete political normality has not yet been attained.

These paragraphs were written with the election results of 1923 and 1927 in mind. The writer went on to predict that as a result of increasing normalisation, the 'cold wind of terror' would no longer prevent PR from having its natural effect—a multiplicity of parties which, after a certain amount of backstairs intrigue, would hammer out a programme that the electorate would never have seen. He ended by urging the government 'while there was still time' to alter the system. At the time when this article was written the Cumann na nGaedheal government might have abolished PR by ordinary law, since the Constitution could be amended by this means during the first eight years after its enactment, and the government had availed itself of this facility to abolish the initiative and to restrict the device of the referendum to constitutional amendments proposed after 22 October, 1930.[42] One minister (Ernest Blythe) had become convinced after 1927 that stable government would never be produced in Ireland by PR, but there does not appear to have been any other voice in the Cabinet to support him. In any case, with such a precarious majority, the government would naturally be deterred from any bold constitutional reform.

In 1932, despite a pre-election merger with the remnants of the National League and some Independents, Cumann na nGaedheal lost 3.4 per cent of the national vote (5 per cent if the National League vote is considered) and five seats, while Fianna Fáil gained 9.3 per cent and fifteen seats. Fianna Fáil won every possible marginal seat, while Labour lost more seats than Cumann na nGaedheal. The combination of a well-balanced programme, intensive organisation, and a new medium for party propaganda, together with the outgoing government's strange courting of unpopularity by introducing an austerity budget on the eve of the election, sufficed to put de Valera at last in the saddle.[43]

De Valera's position was not very secure at first, since he was five seats short of a Dáil majority, but the Labour Party, which had become more and more alienated by the conservatism of Cumann na nGaedheal, gave him its support. Like Cosgrave in 1923, de Valera at once put his policies into effect with a degree of courage and determination not characteristic of minority governments. He engaged in a conflict with the British govern-

26

ment at once on diplomatic and economic levels. By abolishing the oath to the King he was in their eyes unilaterally repudiating the Treaty, and by refusing to pay certain land annuities, also consequent on the Treaty, he invited retaliatory action; the British government soon imposed tariffs on Irish agricultural imports.

The Labour Party was, if anything, more Republican than Fianna Fáil, so the abolition of the oath did not worry it; but the tariffs on agriculture caused immediate distress to farmers and rural workers alike, and Labour enthusiasm for de Valera waned somewhat towards the end of 1932. Cosgrave's party denounced both policies as a breach of national honour. When, towards the end of the year, some Independents, most notably Frank MacDermot and James Dillon,[44] merged with four of the five remaining Farmers' deputies to form a new National Centre Party pledged to settle the Anglo-Irish dispute, Cosgrave made overtures to them to form an anti-Fianna Fáil bloc. But before anything could materialise from the discussions, de Valera dissolved the Dáil during the Christmas recess—a master stroke of strategy.[45]

The 1933 election campaign was the bitterest in the history of the state. The issue as posed by the government was the simple one of a small nation trying to free itself from unwanted ties with a large empire, and on that interpretation the opposition parties, whatever economic arguments they might advance, could be (and were) labelled anti-national. This line of argument brought the Treaty issue, in a somewhat new form, back sharply before the people's minds, and with it came the inevitable concomitant, violence. Militant groups aiming at a complete breach with the British Commonwealth and the reunification of the island by force (known collectively, though inaccurately, as the Irish Republican Army) had remained more or less underground since 1927 when the bulk of their former colleagues had joined Fianna Fáil, and the remaining extremists had lost their seats in the Dáil. The Cosgrave government had proscribed them all and set up a special military tribunal to try cases of illegal possession of arms. On coming to power de Valera revoked the prohibition, and all through 1932 bands of armed men disturbed meetings addressed by members of the former government. During the election campaign, by a natural reaction, Cumann na nGaedheal evolved a rival quasimilitary group, the Army Comrades' Association, which provided bodyguards for ex-ministers and ensured them a hearing.

The Fianna Fáil government used the police force, and in some cases the military, to keep public order during the campaign. Nevertheless the opposition came to rely on their new coadjutors, the ACA, rather than the ordinary guardians of the law.

Although the election was held in the month of January, the worst from a campaigner's point of view, the turnout (80 per cent) has never been higher. The excitement of the campaign and the apparently clear-cut issue between de Valera and Cosgrave transcended all other considerations. De Valera gained five more seats while Cosgrave lost eight—to Fianna Fáil and the Centre Party, which with eleven seats more than filled the gap left by the old Farmers' Party. Fianna Fáil had now exactly half the seats in the Dáil and through an earlier precedent could be assured of the vote of the Ceann Comhairle if a Dáil division should result in a tie.[46]

For the first time a party had secured an overall majority in the Dáil, but by the narrowest possible margin. The stabilising effect of the election result, similar to that of a normal majority decision, was seen in the gradual lessening of tension during the rest of the year; previously a recrudescence of civil war conditions was by no means impossible. Five years later, Professor James Hogan wrote that the year 1933 was the most critical since the civil war and that there was then a grave danger that the country would be plunged into 'Mexican politics,' perhaps for a generation.[47]

The reference is to the strange phenomenon known to Irish history as the 'Blueshirt' movement.[48] After the general election, the ACA was remodelled into a disciplined movement, with a distinctive uniform and a new leader, Dr T. F. O'Higgins (brother of Kevin O'Higgins and a Cumann na nGaedheal deputy), making way for General Eoin O'Duffy. O'Duffy was a founder both of the Free State army—he was Chief of Staff during the civil war—and the police, for he was the first commissioner of the Garda Siochana. Having been dismissed from his post by the government early in 1933, he gravitated into the ACA which was renamed the National Guard, and with a growing, youthful membership, under a military leader, bore an obvious resemblance to contemporary movements in Europe. When the government banned the National Guard in July 1933 (while leaving the IRA paramilitaries untouched), opposition fears of an overthrow of Irish democracy through Fianna Fáil/IRA/communist collusion deepened. In the following month, a merger took place between Cumann na nGaedheal, the Centre Party and the Blueshirts (now appropriately called the League of Youth) to form a new party, the United Ireland Party (Fine Gael), under the presidency of O'Duffy, with Cosgrave, Dillon and Mac-Dermot as vice-presidents. Thus the second largest party in the Free State was now led by a man with no previous political experience and without even a seat in the Dáil.

The alliance lasted barely a year. General O'Duffy had no conception of the responsibilities of a parliamentary leader; with his leanings towards corporativism and his uniformed force he resembled Degrelle or de la Rocque more than Cosgrave or Dillon. When eventually he proposed that farmers withhold land annuities from the government, the more democratic members of the United Ireland Party, led by Professor Hogan, forced his resignation in September 1934.[49] O'Duffy's resignation caused a split in the League of Youth and its gradual decline. At the same time the IRA, whose activities had initially provoked the opposition into forming a counter-movement, was rent by personal quarrels into three groups. Eventually, in 1936, the government banned the IRA, and later both organisations transferred their attentions to Spain where they fought in the civil war—on opposite sides.[50] That was the end of the Blueshirts. In 1935 Cosgrave was elected leader of Fine Gael.

Cosgrave's original intention may have been to strengthen the opposition and so to force an end to the Anglo-Irish 'economic war', which was going on all the time to the great inconvenience of the farmers. Nevertheless, by flirting with an extra-parliamentary, quasi-fascist movement, Cosgrave's party damaged its own prestige, and in effect made it easier for the government to ban extremists both of the Left and the Right. The merger which formed Fine Gael simplified the party structure further. Apart from the two major parties, there remained only the Labour Party, still self-consciously unable to prevent its natural followers from supporting de Valera.

After 1933 de Valera was free to embody his Republican ideals in institutional realities. First of all he eviscerated the Free State Constitution by virtually abolishing the office of Governor General—the oath had already gone—and abolishing the Senate. Then, taking advantage of the abdication of Edward VIII, he removed the Crown completely from the internal affairs of the state, but preserved it as an instrument for external relations in the Executive Authority (External Relations) Act, 1936. By 1937 he had prepared a new Republican Constitution, which he submitted to the people on the same day as the general election in June 1937 (not due until the following year). Its most important innovation was the President of Ireland, who would be the head of the state for internal purposes but have no role in external affairs. The theory of 'external association' implicit in the Constitution was de Valera's own, and he intended to preserve this tenuous relationship with the Commonwealth as a bridge over which the Northern Unionists might eventually walk.[51]

When the Constitution was being debated in the Dáil, Fine Gael opposed it on the ground that the country would be better served by full, unequivocal membership of the Commonwealth, while Labour opposed it because de Valera did not explicitly declare a republic. Before the election was held, the constituencies had been revised (abolishing university seats and nine- and eight-seat constituencies, and almost doubling the number of three-seat divisions) and the increase in the number of three-seat constituencies might have been expected to benefit the government. For the first time only three parties contested the election.

The result of the referendum on the Constitution differed from the election result, if both be considered as plebiscites for or against de Valera: 56.5 per cent of the electorate voted for the Constitution but only 45.2 per cent for Fianna Fáil. In a smaller Dáil (reduced from 153 to 138) the government lost eight seats and its majority. But it was consoled by the knowledge that Fine Gael did not gain any seats and that its votes were proportionately less than the combined Cumann na nGaedheal and Centre Party vote had been in 1933; in fact, the Fine Gael share of the vote wa lower than the Cumann na nGaedheal share in 1932.[52] (Incidentally, Frank MacDermot, who had resigned from Fine Gael in 1935, did not offer himself for re-election.) Fianna Fáil, with almost half the seats in the Dáil, formed a government—again with Labour support—and awaited a suitable opportunity to call another general election.

1938-48

The opportunity came in June 1938 when, after the Anglo-Irish economic war was settled on terms unexpectedly favourable to Eire (the new name for the Irish Free State), a defeat on a snap division in the Dáil gave the government an excuse to go to the country. Fine Gael was badly in need of a counter-policy but merely criticised the Anglo-Irish trade agreement, apparently for no better reason than that it had been negotiated by Fianna Fáil! During the campaign the electoral system was raised as a party issue for the first time. To understand how this came about it is necessary to recapitulate a little.

When de Valera presented his draft constitution to the Dáil in 1937 it differed from the previous one in one important respect as far as the electoral system was concerned: whereas the Free State Constitution merely prescribed 'the principles' of Proportional Representation, Article 16 of the new Constitution prescribed the single transferable vote. When this article was being debated, the ex-Attorney General (subsequently Taoiseach), John A. Costello, asking why the change had been made, suggested that the Constitution be left more flexible and the details of the electoral system be relegated, as before, to the sphere of ordinary legislation. Costello did not find fault with the system but thought that the country should not be tied to it indefinitely: if a change were needed he saw it would obviously be more difficult once the system was entrenched in the Constitution.[53]

De Valera's reply was quite logical. He thought that the electoral system was too important to leave at the mercy of ordinary political warfare. If it could be changed by law it would provide a temptation for a government to try to manipulate it to its own advantage, as the government of Northern Ireland had done. It is worth noting that while the only frontal attack on the system during the debates was made by a Fianna Fáil back-bencher, the Fine Gael spokesmen did not express any great affection for it, and the Costello amendment, if passed, would have made it much easier for either party to alter the system, provided it commanded a majority of the House.[54] The first misgivings of the Cosgrave party regarding PR have been referred to already. Subsequently a proposal was made, at the first Ard Fheis of the reorganised party (1935), that they should commit themselves to abolishing the system, but it did not command sufficient support in the National Executive and was dropped. Nevertheless in the party organ, *United Ireland* (7 February 1935), the same charge was made as in *The Star* five years earlier, that PR was originally foisted on the country by the British, and by the PR Society 'who wanted to try out its nostrum on the dog'.

Thus, for the first fifteen years de Valera appears to have favoured the Irish form of PR, or at least to have thought that its advantages outweighed its disadvantages; he paid a tribute to the successful working of the system during the debate on Article 16 of the Constitution. At the same time, some at least of the leading members of Cosgrave's party came to dislike the fissiparous effects of PR, and while their feeling was not sufficiently strong to swing the party against the system there was no question, up to the end of 1937, of Cumann na nGaedheal or Fine Gael being committed to its retention; the Costello amendment, indeed, pointed the other way. The smaller parties did not concern themselves with the system until it was challenged. The first sign of a change in the party line-up came after a speech delivered by de Valera on 2 June 1938 at Kilrush, during the election campaign.

In the Kilrush speech de Valera adverted to the possibility that that election, like the previous one, would fail to give any party an overall majority. If the parliamentary stalemate which had persisted since 1927 (except for the four years 1933-7) were to be prolonged by a series of inconclusive elections, parliamentary government might well be endangered. The government, he said, ought to be formed from the party that polled the largest number of votes. De Valera did not specify any alternative to PR but by implication favoured the majority system.[55]

The speech produced an instant reaction. Labour found in the suggestion a direct threat to its own existence as a small sectional party, and Fine Gael, forgetting its former doubts and misgivings about Irish PR, sprang to the defence of the system as a bulwark against 'one-party dictatorship', to which it claimed de Valera was secretly aspiring. Both the non-government dailies vehemently opposed any alteration of the system. The *Irish Times* ran a headline, 'Premier's Threat to PR', and its leading article said that 'Proportional Representation had been Southern Ireland's answer to all hostile criticism' for sixteen years; as a result of it 'minorities have obtained seats in Parliament which they would not have had a hope of obtaining under the block vote'.[56]

It is hard to guess what minorities the *Irish Times* had in mind unless it meant Labour and the Farmers. As has already been shown, the interest with which the *Irish Times* had traditionally been associated, the Southern Unionists, had not secured separate representation in the Dáils elected since 1922, although they had built up a party in the Senate. The *Irish Times* admitted that no party had secured a majority since 1927 (it might have said since 1922) but it pleaded that only once had a government been defeated on a major issue. Still, the course of events since 1927 gave few grounds for hoping that that state of affairs would continue. To the question of what political solution could be found if the 1938 election were also to prove inconclusive, the *Irish Times* could only offer the suggestion

31

of a national (all-party) government on the dubious model of the Mac-Donald-Baldwin coalition of 1931—a most unlikely contingency in view of the bitter hostility between the two major parties.

For the next two weeks the correspondence columns of the *Irish Times* were filled with letters on the subject, mainly in defence of PR. John H. Humphreys contributed his piece, but the letter which above all others created the impression that the former Southern Unionists were thoroughly satisfied with PR came from the Rev. Canon A.A. Luce, Professor of Moral Philosophy at Trinity College, Dublin and a world-famous authority on the philosophy of Bishop Berkeley.[57] Canon Luce began by saying that he had previously written when Fine Gael was attacking PR, but that was just 'a vague and passing feeling of dissatisfaction.' He continued:

It would be a thousand pities if the other great party, in a fit of impatience, were to scrap this well-tested instrument of enlightened democracy, an instrument to which we all, irrespective of creed, class and party, owe far more than we sometimes realise, and which can do for our children what it has done for us.

'PR' has been a healing force in our midst. Old political feuds are dying; public spirit is replacing faction. Our elections are well-conducted. The voice of reason is heard and the gun is silent. 'PR' deserves much of the credit; for 'PR' produces contented and loyal minorities, whereas the other system breeds muzzled, sullen, discontented minorities, predisposed to doctrines of violence.

The letter ended with the strange proposition that a government with a majority of six under PR is 'infinitely stronger' than one with a majority of sixty 'elected otherwise'. No explanation was offered.

Canon Luce's letter has been much more widely publicised than an examination of its contents would warrant. The lofty judgments contained in it do not stand up when confronted with the evidence even then available. Where in 1938 were the 'discontented minorities predisposed to doctrines of violence'? Certainly not in Great Britain or the Commonwealth countries using 'the other system'. If anywhere, they were in the European countries with highly proportional systems. The history of the Weimar Republic and of Italy between 1918 and 1922 does not reveal the existence of 'loyal and contented minorities', but rather the exact opposite. Canon Luce's predictions about Irish conditions were much too optimistic. The 'old political feud' between Fianna Fáil and Fine Gael was good for many more years, and although the gun had been silent for at least two years, the subversive organisations were at that very time preparing a new campaign of violence in England to focus attention on 'Partition'.

Professor Hogan contributed a letter (referred to above) of a very different tenor from that of Canon Luce. He wrote that those who regarded with unconcern the prospect of another stalemate were overlooking the dangerous conditions in which they lived. Between 1927 and 1932 the two major parties were running neck and neck; 1933 was the most critical year since the civil war, but when de Valera secured a working majority tension at once relaxed.

The lesson of our political experience since the Civil War is unmistakable. It was not in any measure due to Proportional Representation, but definitely in spite of it, that the State was safely tided over the most critical years . . . We can thank our lucky stars that Proportional Representation did not get the chance of plunging the country into Mexican politics, perhaps, for a generation.[58]

Faced with a formidable opposition and unwilling to give fresh ammunition to Fine Gael and Labour, de Valera backed down, pointing out that since PR was enshrined in the Constitution it could not be removed without a referendum. That was not strictly true, since the Constitution, like its predecessor, provided that for the first three years of its existence (actually dating from the election of the first President of Ireland) it might be amended by ordinary law, though afterwards a referendum would be necessary.[59] Nevertheless, the election results were to show that Fianna Fáil, on a simple estimate of party strength, had a better chance of winning a referendum in 1938 than at any time before or since. For de Valera won an absolute majority of the votes cast (52 per cent)—an extremely rare achievement under any electoral system—and an overall majority of fifteen seats, while Fine Gael lost three seats and Labour four (out of thirteen, although Labour secured the same proportion of the poll as in the previous year). But the size of his majority removed the very reason de Valera had advanced for changing the system, so no more was heard for the time being about the disadvantages of Irish PR. It is clear that de Valera's change of heart goes back at least to 1937, and possibly earlier. It is quite possible that he included PR in the draft Constitution through a fear that otherwise the combined force of the opposition might secure its defeat at the 1937 plebiscite, and the fundamental law obviously took priority over the electoral system.[60]

The year 1937 marked the end of the era in which elections were personal plebiscites between de Valera and Cosgrave. In 1938 Fine Gael put up seventy-six candidates (compared with ninety-five in the previous election) and if it were to form a single-party government, almost all of them would have to be elected. Moreover, the successful conclusion of the 'Economic War' badly upset Fine Gael's morale and its opposition to the new agreement seemed irreconcilable with its former policy.

There were more far-reaching reasons for Fine Gael's inability to make the pendulum swing back in its favour during the first six controversial years of Fianna Fáil rule. Most obvious was the decline in the quality of the party elite through the premature death or defeat at the polls of its most dynamic leaders: Kevin O'Higgins, Cosgrave's first deputy leader, was assassinated in 1927; Patrick Hogan, the brilliant Minister for Agriculture, was killed in a car accident in 1936; Ernest Blythe and Desmond FitzGerald lost their seats in 1933-7. The Blueshirt episode also adversely affected the party's prestige, although it provided the occasion for James Dillon (the most valuable acquisition of the party during these years) to join Fine Gael.

But these gaps on the front bench might have been filled easily enough had Fine Gael possessed a mass organisation constantly recruiting and training young men for the time when the ageing Treaty generation would hand over the reins. Instead, outside the largest cities and towns the Fine Gael organisation existed only on paper—and what Warner Moss had written approvingly (in 1933) on its capacity for underground organisation still held good:

> Sometimes Cosgrave's opponents did not realise that his party was actively engaged in campaign work. Cosgrave's party, Cumann na nGaedheal, often carried its organisation into new areas by merely sending letters to influential men asking their aid. They went about quietly, often making use of social groups which already existed . . . [61]

The method of 'making use of social groups which already existed' might have worked well enough when Cumann na nGaedheal was invested with the authority and prestige of government, but proved much too tenuous and insubstantial when Fine Gael was faced with the problem of attracting younger voters to fill the inevitably increasing gaps that time would leave in the ranks of its original supporters, not to speak of winning back those who had gone over to Fianna Fáil. The Fianna Fáil organisation, on the other hand, remained firmly based on the local cumann.

After 1938 de Valera was as supreme in Ireland as any democratic leader could be. He had vanquished his rival Cosgrave in four successive elections; he had outbidden Labour for the support of the working classes, and he had built up his party into a formidable machine in which enthusiasm was combined with unflinching loyalty to the leader. Now that his Republican goals had been attained and the ambitious social programme (health and unemployment relief, cottages for labourers and so on) had been implemented, his policies took on an increasingly conservative colour which rendered it harder than ever for Fine Gael to win back the propertied classes; these by now were quite satisfied with Fianna Fáil.

The outbreak of war in 1939 also worked in de Valera's favour. He proclaimed Ireland's neutrality, thus putting Cosgrave into a further dilemma, since the pro-Commonwealth leanings of Fine Gael ought naturally to have made it advocate full cooperation in the struggle in which the very life of the Commonwealth was at stake.[62] For Fine Gael to set itself against neutrality in the face of Fianna Fáil's enormous majority would not only be futile, but also might result in a further loss of popularity to the party and a prolongation of its stay in the wilderness. On the other hand, 'for Fine Gael to accept and endorse the logic of neutrality would be tantamount to abandoning the Commonwealth idea, which would be to forfeit the main ground of its individuality as a party. For once it ceased to stand for a Commonwealth policy, no simple and fundamental issue would remain to distinguish the Fine Gael party from its former rival'.[63]

Besides forcing Cosgrave to discard, at least temporarily, his most distinctive policy, the war resulted in a natural closing of the party ranks. The Constitution was amended by vote of the Oireachtas to enable the government to cope with the emergency by numerous ministerial orders. What was greatly feared was that the IRA, then conducting a campaign of bomb-throwing and arson in England, would try to force the country into the war against England; some of them even went as emissaries to Germany. De Valera could claim that by adhering to a strict policy of neutrality he was acting in the best interests of the Allies, since, should he attempt to involve the country with Britain against Germany, the IRA was sufficiently powerful and the memories of the Anglo-Irish struggle sufficiently vivid to enable it to sabotage the national effort.

During the war years the area of political controversy was increasingly narrowed: the rationing of newsprint and political censorship of the newspapers (in the interests of neutrality), together with the pressure of outside events, hindered Fine Gael and Labour from exercising their normal functions as an opposition. Nevertheless, two general elections were fought during this period, in 1943 and 1944. (Sweden was the only other European democracy to experience a war-time election.) The election of 1943 was noted for the slogan, 'Don't change horses when crossing the stream', an argument for the continuation in power of the eleven-year-old government, and for the first electoral test of a new farmers' party, Clann na Talmhan (children of the land). This party was founded by a Galway farmer, Michael Donnellan, shortly after the general election of 1938. It was largely concentrated in the west of Ireland—unlike the former Farmers' Party—and was concerned with articulating the interests of the small farmers, which it was claimed were being neglected by Fianna Fáil.[64]

The newspapers were restricted by newsprint rationing to a minimum of political comment and the candidates, through scarcity of petrol, to a minimum of public meetings. The results showed, however, that these factors, although affecting all, did not militate against the two smaller parties as might have been expected. For, while Fianna Fáil lost ten seats and its majority, Fine Gael lost thirteen, the gainers being Labour, which won eight seats and had a larger number of deputies than at any time since June 1927, and the new farmers' party, which for a sectional group did very well on its first showing, with 10 per cent of the votes and thirteen seats. Fianna Fáil's long tenure of office had naturally provoked a reaction, and the result was more typical of PR than at any election since 1927. The Treaty issue had become obsolete and no new issue had appeared to crystallise the electorate behind the two major parties.

Neutrality was adhered to by Fine Gael to such an extent that the deputy leader, James Dillon, was expelled from the party in 1942 for advocating the entry of the country into the war on the side of the Allies. There now remained no distinctive policy to characterise Fine Gael, and that lack, added to neglect of the party organisation and supine leadership, resulted in an electoral debacle—a loss of 10 per cent in votes by comparison with the 1938 figures. Among the front-benchers to lose their seats were two ex-ministers and the future Taoiseach, John Costello.[65]

By comparison with 1937 Fianna Fáil had sustained a greater loss, since it was now in a minority of five. At the opening of the Dáil, Clann na Talmhan voted for de Valera's re-election as Taoiseach, which gave him a majority, but he chafed as much at dependence on them as on Labour in 1932-3, and his speeches made clear his hardening attitude towards PR and an express intention to make another appeal to the country at the most favourable opportunity. The conditions were speedily realised. A formal request (early in 1944) from the British and American representatives in Dublin that Eire break off diplomatic relations with Germany and Japan was enough to jolt the public into realising that the danger of involvement in the war—very real in 1940 and 1941, but rather remote from the beginning of 1942—was not quite so distant as they had thought, and the slightest suggestion of war neurosis was bound to help the government. The two main opposition parties were seen at an increasing disadvantage vis-à-vis Fianna Fáil. Even if they were to coalesce there was little hope of reducing de Valera's great lead, and although Labour had become more and more antagonistic to Fianna Fáil, it was largely because Fianna Fáil policy was becoming indistinguishable from that of the 'capitalist' Fine Gael. By and large Labour voters' lower preferences still went to Fianna Fáil.

In addition to the virtual certainty that another general election would return a Fianna Fáil government, the cause of the opposition parties was worsened by the retirement in January 1944 of W. T. Cosgrave from the Fine Gael leadership—and the fact that his successor, General Richard Mulcahy, was then without a seat in the Dáil. A split in the Labour movement was an added disadvantage.

This episode is much too complex to be adequately treated here.[66] Suffice it to say that the Labour recovery (especially in Dublin where it became the largest party in the municipal elections of 1942) occurred at a time when government legislation imposing a wage freeze was causing widespread resentment among the unions. This led to a number of longtime dissidents, including James Larkin and his son, seeking re-admission to the party. ('Big Jim' had been an Independent Labour TD from 1937 to 1938.) In 1943 both Larkins were nominated as official Labour candidates in Dublin, despite strenuous opposition from within the party led by Larkin's old enemy, William O'Brien. The Larkins were elected, but in January 1944 the ITGWU disaffiliated from the Labour Party on the ground of 'communist infiltration'; and of the eight Labour deputies who were members of that union, five seceded and formed a new party called National Labour.[67]

A defeat in the Dáil after a snap division on a minor issue in May 1944 gave de Valera the excuse he needed to call a new election. Excepting Fianna Fáil whose machine was effectively geared to the campaign, the other parties fought languidly and without enthusiasm. After a short campaign and an apathetic poll—the turnout, 68.5 per cent, was the lowest since 1927—Fianna Fáil won an overall majority for the third time. All the other parties fared worse than in 1943. The new farmers' party maintained its share of the vote but dropped two seats. The two Labour factions fought against each other and won only twelve seats altogether (eight Labour, four National Labour) compared with seventeen in 1943; among the losers was Larkin Senior. Fine Gael was reduced from thirty-two to thirty seats; it had nominated a mere fifty-five candidates, possibly because a number of former Fine Gael deputies and candidates were now standing as Independents. Two of them who had lost their seats in 1943 again failed at the polls, but the Cork industrialist, Mr William O'Dwyer, who had run on the same ticket as Cosgrave in the previous year, now topped the poll as an Independent, thus ensuring a loss of one seat to his former party. The net result was that Fianna Fáil won back all but one of the seats lost in 1943.

The result of the 1944 election showed that even after a longer term in office than Cosgrave's party had experienced, Fianna Fáil was still by far the most popular party and the existing opposition parties seemed totally unable either to coalesce or to win seats from it. Even the *Irish Independent*, which had faithfully supported Fine Gael through the years, had to admit that the result of the 1944 election was conclusive.[68]

The poor condition of the opposition served to enhance the apparent invincibility of the government. The squabble within the ranks of Labour had cost it all the advantage gained in 1943, and the new farmers' party did not look as if it would be any more successful than the old. Fine Gael seemed to be in a rapid decline. The return to the Dáil in 1944 of the new leader, General Mulcahy, and of the future Taoiseach, J. A. Costello, was inadequate consolation for another fall in voting strength and a net loss of two seats. The organisation in the country seemed moribund. In November 1944, following the appointment of Fionan Lynch (a survivor of Cosgrave's government) as a Circuit Court Judge, the Fine Gael candidate in the South Kerry by-election was beaten into third place by Clann na Talmhan. In December 1945, four by-elections were held on the same day, three of them without Fine Gael candidates—the party had not won a by-election for ten years—and some observers predicted the party's speedy demise.[69]

Before leaving this period it is worth mentioning that in the elections of 1943 and 1944 other minor parties stood but failed to secure election.

Two were obscure Republican groups, Coras na Poblachta and Ailtiri na hAiseirghe, which left behind them a trail of lost deposits; but the Monetary Reform Party merits a footnote to history, since it was under its auspices that Oliver J. Flanagan began, in 1943, his long association with Laois-Offaly, although from the time of his election he comported himself as an Independent.[70]

1948-57

The end of the war and a return to normal political conditions found Fianna Fáil in a complacent mood. Fearing little from their existing rivals, ministers, to judge by their utterances, regarded themselves as permanent as civil servants. But this complacency was rudely shaken by the appearance in 1946 of a new party, Clann na Poblachta (the children of the republic), led by Sean MacBride, a lawyer, both of whose parents had played a prominent part in the Anglo-Irish struggle, and who had himself been a leader of the IRA in the 1930s.[71] The policy of the new party was a blend of left-wing economics (higher social services and guaranteed wage rates) and doctrinaire republicanism (repeal of the External Relations Act and severance of the link with British currency), which somewhat resembled Fianna Fáil policy of the late twenties.

The main appeal of Clann na Poblachta lay, however, in its professed intention to get away from the *damnosa hereditas* of the civil war, the irreconcilability of Fianna Fáil and Fine Gael, and to study national problems objectively. This would win over the uncommitted mature voters, while the rekindling of Republican ardours which had cooled under Fianna Fáil was especially attractive to the young.

Although it must not be exaggerated, the dual mission of Clann na Poblachta was very evident in its early years. MacBride wanted to win for his party the widest measure of popular support by promising a fresh and objective approach to politics; at the same time, both in its constitution and personnel the party was committed to an isolationist foreign policy, or at least an anti-British one. Many of MacBride's closest associates were survivors of the civil war who had refused to join de Valera in 1927, or who broke with him when he suppressed the IRA in 1936. They also denounced the repressive measures taken by the government during the war.[72]

The new party had a snowball effect. Within a very short time MacBride was able to build up constituency associations all over the country, and in November 1947 he felt strong enough to challenge Fianna Fáil in three by-elections, two of which he won, Fine Gael being relegated to third place.

De Valera still had a comfortable overall majority and the Twelfth Dáil had eighteen months of life left. Nevertheless, he decided to dissolve immediately rather than wait for the new party to consolidate its gains. Shortly before the elections the constituencies had again been revised under Article 16.2.4 of the Constitution, which prescribed a revision at least once in every twelve years, with due regard to changes in distribution of the population: the seven-seat divisions had been abolished, the number of three-seat constituencies increased, and the number of deputies raised from 138 to 147.

The election of February 1948 was a very curious one. To most outside observers, and to not a few at home, the struggle appeared to be between the old, tired and previously immovable Fianna Fáil and the young, enthusiastic, and rapidly developing radical party.[73] MacBride's own speeches were cautious and restrained, but the by-election successes had gone so much to the heads of his followers that they talked of repeating the 1918 landslide and forming a government on their own. This over-optimism gave Fianna Fáil the excuse to warn the electorate against entrusting power to a new and inexperienced party. Moreover, the immaturity of the Clann na Poblachta organisation was shown in the variety of candidatures (of which a lack of political experience was the most common characteristic) and the imprudence of nominating at least two candidates to every constituency, which strained its resources excessively. With ninety-three candidates Clann na Poblachta fielded the largest number next to Fianna Fáil. Fine Gael put up eighty-two candidates, but fought a low-key campaign. Its erosion of support had continued; one deputy from a midland constituency resigned from the party in 1947 for reasons that were by no means clear from his resignation statement—he sat on as an Independent and rejoined Fine Gael in 1952; another sitting deputy stood in 1948 as an Independent; and three died during the campaign. So a mere twenty-two outgoing Fine Gael deputies contested the 1948 election—less than half the number elected in 1938. (Virtually the only new Fine Gael deputies elected since then had been sons of previous TDs—most notably Liam Cosgrave elected for Dublin County in 1943).[74]

Although the split in the Labour movement had been rendered less personalised by the death of 'Big Jim' Larkin in 1947, the two separate parties again contested the election, the main Labour Party—in which incidentally 'Young Jim' Larkin, who had been re-elected in 1944, again stood as an official party candidate—led by William Norton (who had succeeded to the leadership in 1932) and National Labour led by James Everett, a long-standing Labour deputy, first elected in 1922. The total number of candidates (405) was the highest ever.

When the votes were counted it was seen that in a turnout identical to that of 1943, Fianna Fáil got exactly the same share of the national vote (41.9 per cent), but secured a lower share of the seats. In the new Dáil, containing 147 seats instead of 138, it secured sixty-seven seats. Fine Gael fell below its 1944 percentage of votes—for the first time it secured less than 20 per cent—but gained one seat. The congratulatory tone of the editorials in the Dublin newspapers ('The remarkably firm stand by Fine Gael', 'Fine Gael polled well')[75] showed that they expected an electoral debacle for that party!

Both Labour parties secured almost identical shares of the poll as in 1944 but did much better in terms of seats—National Labour increasing its Dáil strength from four to five, while Official Labour went up from eight to fourteen seats. Clann na Talmhan showed a drastic falling-off of support and lost four seats. But the most remarkable feature of the election was the fate of Clann na Poblachta. Their candidates won 13.2 per cent of the vote—less than their more optimistic predictions, but still the highest ever won by a party at its first attempt, and a higher proportion than any minor party had ever won (excepting Labour in 1943). But while the new party secured a much higher share of the poll than Labour it won a mere ten seats to Labour's fourteen. Proportionately, the Clann should have won nineteen seats, and an examination of the results shows that putting up too many candidates was a disastrous electoral strategy. No less than ten Clann candidates were runners-up in their constituencies, and many thousands of votes were lost on transfer.[76]

The only alternative government to Fianna Fáil was a coalition of the other five parties; even then they would need the support of several Independents to command a majority. The Fine Gael leader, General Mulcahy, at once started discussions between the parties and eventually the smaller parties agreed to subordinate their ancient dislike of Fine Gael to the desire to put de Valera out and hold office themselves. By 18 February they had mustered sufficient support for a ten-point programme of a most general and unexceptionable character, and for a Fine Gael Taoiseach, not Mulcahy, but the ex-Attorney General, John A. Costello, who had never held ministerial office.[77] The five parties were allocated ministries roughly in proportion to their Dáil membership. Only two had previously held ministerial office, Mulcahy and Patrick McGilligan.[78]

The formation of the first Coalition initiated a new era in Irish politics. The number of participating parties was so great and their characteristic policies were so diverse, the majority of the government was so precarious and the opposition so large and solid, that at first only a short life expectancy could be predicted. But after the first few months they were able to breathe freely. A modus vivendi was attained by avoiding any legislation that might involve the loss of even one deputy's support, and by introducing measures that were likely to enhance ministerial popularity, especially by increasing public expenditure. Undoubtedly, there was far less of a sense of collective responsibility among ministers than in any single-party government, and although (with the exception of the two Clann na Poblachta ministers) ministers of different parties frequently appeared on the same platform to demonstrate their solidarity, their speeches showed that many of them (especially the party leaders) ran their departments much as they pleased, and also often made public pronouncements on matters which fell within the responsibilities of other ministers.[79] There is some evidence that Costello tried to be an impartial chairman, but faced with so many indispensable colleagues with such varying views, his position would be impossible in the event of a Cabinet crisis.[80] The only cohesive force in the government was the fear of de Valera.

Apart from attractive money-spending schemes the most memorable incidents under the Coalition were the breaking of the last link with the Commonwealth and the formal declaration of a republic for the Twenty-Six Counties, and the Dr Noel Browne episode—which led to the Coalition's downfall after three-and-a-quarter years in office.

The events leading up to the passing of the Republic of Ireland Act (1949) form a bizarre postscript to the constitutional evolution between 1922 and 1937. External association with the Commonwealth had long represented de Valera's desire for a compromise between the Republican and pro-British traditions of South and North. The constitutional issue had not been raised at the 1948 election except by MacBride, and he had afterwards categorically admitted that he had received no popular mandate.[81] However, without any previous warning, Costello announced (at a press conference at the end of a visit to Canada, on 7 September 1948) that the constitutional position was anomalous and in need of revision.[82] The bill to confer the remaining attributes of sovereignty on the Irish President (the power to appoint and receive diplomatic representatives) passed through the Dáil in November with scarcely any opposition, de Valera supporting the motion for a second reading.[83]

The consequences were, first, an immediate general election for Stormont on the perennial 'Ulster in danger' cry. In spite of (or perhaps because of) an all-party drive in Dublin to provide funds for the Nationalists in Northern Ireland, the Unionists won four extra seats and the Northern Ireland Labour Party, which had fared well in 1945, received a setback from which it did not recover until 1958.[84] The second result was that the British Labour government introduced a bill which prescribed that the constitutional position of Northern Ireland could not be changed without the consent of its parliament; the passing of this bill occasioned vehement but futile outbursts in Dublin.[85] Lastly, there was a recrudescence of subversive activities. The IRA had been quiescent in the last years of de Valera's rule and the Fine Gael Minister for Justice took the risk of releasing several IRA members who had been interned during the war in the hope of 'taking the gun out of politics'. But by focusing public attention on Anglo-Irish relations the government provided the revolutionaries with the excuse for starting a new propaganda campaign against the Six Counties. When a member of the Dáil started to form a private army for that purpose the government was too weak to do anything but ignore him. Nor did it attempt to stop the subversives from holding public meetings, especially in Dublin.

The famous 'Mother and Child' scheme of 1951 and the crisis it precipitated have often been described, and may be summarised very briefly. The Clann na Poblachta Minister for Health, Dr Noel Browne, was encountering stiff opposition from the medical profession towards his free-for-all

41

scheme for ante-natal care, when it became known that the Catholic hierarchy were also opposed on moral grounds (1950).[86] When the matter was debated in Cabinet, opinion appears to have been unanimous that the scheme should be withdrawn, but Browne continued to advertise it publicly. Eventually MacBride (arrogating to himself one of the constitutional functions of the Taoiseach) demanded Browne's resignation, which Browne tendered in what was a masterly piece of invective—at the same time releasing the relevant correspondence to all the newspapers (11 April 1951).[87] The Browne resignation and the ensuing Dáil debates were extremely damaging to the prestige of the Coalition.[88]

These were the worst possible conditions for an election, and there is no evidence that the government intended dissolving at this time. But their hand was forced; in May two Independent farmers defected, because of a refusal by the government to raise the price of milk; and with their Dáil majority in ruins the Coalition had to go to the country that same month.

The 1951 election was the first genuine 'pork-barrel' election in Ireland. Although the break with the Commonwealth, the Browne resignation, and the weakness and lack of responsibility of the government which they revealed, were fresh in everyone's mind, they were scarcely mentioned from election platforms on either side. Both the Coalition and Fianna Fáil speakers concentrated their fire on promises the other side had made to reduce the cost of living, and both produced material inducements of various kinds to swing the uncommitted voters. But there was the occasional reference to Fine Gael's 'betrayal' of those voters who valued the Commonwealth connection.[89]

In a turnout slightly higher than in 1948, Fianna Fáil gained 4.4 per cent of the vote, but so solidly did the voters for the various coalition parties support each other's candidates that the usual 'bonus' won by the largest party was not forthcoming and Fianna Fáil increased its representation by just one seat (0.7 per cent). The attainment of office after so many years in the wilderness had obviously helped Fine Gael. Its six outgoing ministers all improved their position, and the party gained almost 6 per cent of the votes and nine seats, mainly at the expense of their Coalition partners. Clann na Talmhan lost one seat, and was now confined to four constituencies in Connacht. The two wings of Labour had been reunited in 1950, under Norton's leadership, but although the single party's share of the vote was almost the same as the combined share of Labour and National Labour in 1948, they suffered a net loss of three seats. Clann na Poblachta was the worst hit; its share of the vote fell by two-thirds, and it held just two seats. Apparently the Mother and Child crisis harmed his former party more than the ex-minister, Noel Browne; for while MacBride scraped home on the last count in his Dublin constituency, Browne was elected on the first count and another ex-Clann deputy, Jack McQuillan (who had resigned from the party in sympathy with Browne), was also returned.

Fianna Fáil was six seats short of a majority, but when the new Dáil assembled, the outgoing Ceann Comhairle (Speaker), Frank Fahy, who had held the office since 1932, did not offer himself for re-election, and a Labour deputy was elected in his place.[90] That meant a net gain of two seats to Fianna Fáil, and de Valera was elected Taoiseach with the support of four Independents, including Browne.

This was not the kind of parliamentary situation that appealed to de Valera, but there was no alternative source of support, nor any advantage to be gained from a snap election; for unlike the situation in the late 1930s and early 1940s, a viable alternative government was in the offing. This was pointedly demonstrated by Costello, the ex-Taoiseach, assuming the role of Leader of the Opposition—not Mulcahy, who remained leader of the Fine Gael party. Apart from promoting some long-serving back-benchers to ministerial office, de Valera did nothing noteworthy during this administration. In 1952 three of the four Independents (including Browne) who had supported de Valera's re-election in 1951 joined Fianna Fáil; but this was offset by the admission of three Independents, including James Dillon and Oliver Flanagan, into the ranks of Fine Gael.[91]

The weakness of this *immobiliste,* minority government was shown in 1953 when farmers' organisations arranged a national milk strike, which lasted for some weeks. But more important was the trend evidenced in by-elections. Fianna Fáil had held its own during 1952; but two by-elections in 1953 had been won by Fine Gael; and in March 1954, Fine Gael won two more by-elections, in Cork and Louth. Although there was no change in the balance of parties in the Dáil (since the by-elections were occasioned by the deaths of two Fine Gael deputies) a startling increase in the Fine Gael share of the vote persuaded de Valera to call a general election, in May 1954.

The style of the 1954 election was very similar to that of 1951. Although the former Coalition parties campaigned independently, it was understood that if they won a majority of seats another 'inter-party' arrangement would follow. Apart from this, there was no issue in the election, and, as in 1951, both sides vied with each other in dangling promises of material benefits before the electorate. The essentially parochial character of this type of electioneering may be illustrated by one example. In 1951 Fianna Fáil widely distributed a leaflet showing how the prices of essential commodities had risen under the Coalition—with no mention of the Korean War and its effect on import prices. In 1954 Fine Gael took its revenge by reproducing the same leaflet, with prices adjusted—upwards, of course—to the current level.[92] Foreign affairs were totally ignored in 1954, as in 1951.

The 1954 election produced a further party simplification. Fianna Fáil lost three seats and all hope of staying in office; Fine Gael gained another ten seats; Labour another two; Clann na Poblachta went up to three, but Clann na Talmhan declined further to five seats.

Costello formed another coalition with Labour and Clann na Talmhan support, but the latter was now very much the junior partner. MacBride did not accept office but gave the government his support.

At first this Coalition seemed more stable than its predecessor since the three participating parties controlled a Dáil majority. There had been built up a positive alternative to Fianna Fáil, and the two major coalition partners, Fine Gael and Labour, had greatly enhanced their position. Fine Gael had been given a new lease of life by its accession to office in 1948. The party, making up for the torpor of former years, appointed a full-time organiser and built up flourishing local associations, especially directed to the young—an element which in the past had consistently been neglected.[93] In the general election of 1948 Fine Gael had dropped below 20 per cent of the total poll; in the election of 1954 it went up to 32 per cent. The re-united Labour Party now had eighteen seats.

Yet the prospects of the second Coalition, so favourable in 1954, were brought to ruin by two causes: first, a worsening of the balance of trade in 1956 forced the (Fine Gael) Minister for Finance, Gerard Sweetman, to impose a regime of economic austerity, which largely dispelled the illusions fostered by six years of comfortable living; second, the IRA campaign against 'Partition', which had been waged at the propaganda level ever since 1948, erupted in 1955 into a series of daring guerrilla raids across the border. For a whole year the government tried to play down the existence of the raids, but when, at the end of December 1956, some policemen and raiders were killed and the danger of civil war loomed again, Costello promised (6 January 1957) that the full resources of the state would be used to prevent further raids. Soon (29 January) MacBride's party withdrew its support, and rather than face a vote of 'no confidence' already proposed by Fianna Fáil (on economic grounds), the second Coalition came to an end after less than three years in office.

The campaign of February 1957 was waged in an atmosphere resembling that of 1933 and earlier.[94] The IRA raids, although futile and nihilistic, had aroused the latent patriotic feelings of many of the electors, and a new party claiming to be the lineal descendants of the first Sinn Féin named nineteen candidates, including relatives of the dead guerrillas. Both Fianna Fáil and Fine Gael tried to avoid the delicate problem of what policy to adopt in regard to the IRA after the election. But the accumulated effects of financial austerity and the government's loss of prestige through its handling of the subversive problem caused a swing back to Fianna Fáil of 5 per cent of the vote: for the first time since 1948 it won the lower preferences of Coalition supporters and came back with seventy-eight seats, an overall majority of ten, and de Valera formed his last administration. Fine Gael lost the ten seats gained in 1954; Labour lost seven; Clann na Talmhan two; and Clann na Poblachta two, including that of MacBride, who had been the efficient cause of the dissolution. The turnout was 5 per cent lower than in 1954. Sinn Féin won 5.3 per cent of the vote and four seats. In Sligo-Leitrim their successful candidate headed the poll; in Longford-Westmeath Rory Brady, later to become President of Provisional Sinn Féin, was elected; and in Monaghan a brother of one of the dead guerrillas was returned. Three of the Sinn Féin gains were from Fianna Fáil and the fourth from an ex-Fianna Fáil Independent.

This was an impressive achievement—the first seats won under the Sinn Féin label since June 1927;[95] but it appears to have been on a sympathy vote which was not easily sustained. The Sinn Féin deputies refused to take their seats, and when the party contested a by-election in Dublin the following November the wave of sympathy was seen to have subsided, and the candidate lost his deposit.

Another interesting feature of the election was the return to the Dáil of Dr Browne. He had lost his seat in Dublin South-East as an outgoing Fianna Fáil candidate in 1954, and since then had quarrelled with the party. In 1957 he was elected as an Independent, for the second time.[96]

6
The First Referendum on PR (1959)

In 1948 the *Sunday Independent* had first raised the rumour that the Twenty-Six Counties would soon be declared a republic, and in so doing had probably forced Costello's hand.[1] Thereafter the paper group had pointedly refrained from editorial comment on the major controversial issues.[2]

Ten years after its famous scoop on the Republic, the *Independent* presented its readers with another. On 28 August 1958 the political correspondent of the *Irish Independent* reported that 'a strong feeling existed' among politicians that PR might soon be abolished. He added that, although many in Fianna Fáil were dissatisfied with the system, he believed 'quite a few members of the opposition are not too keen on it either' and quoted an unidentified deputy's remark that 'it may now be said to have become a demoralising system'.

The same day the Government Information Bureau, under pressure from journalists, revealed that the government would give 'full and early consideration' to the question of abolishing PR and that this would be done in connection with the constituency revision which would fall due again in 1959.[3]

At once the *Irish Times* took up the cudgels on behalf of PR. Admitting that the single transferable vote had not afforded the practical protection to minorities which was the reason for its adoption, in mitigation of its weaknesses the editorial asked what other system had not displayed more? The *Irish Times* editorial quickly disposed of the arguments against PR: as far as strong government was concerned, de Valera's majority was proportionately stronger than Macmillan's, and very few Irish governments had commanded so small a majority as to be positively insecure; moreover, there were fewer parties then than in the early years of the state. Searching for an ulterior motive, the *Irish Times* found it in the prospect, 'however vague', of de Valera's eventual retirement, which might have panicked his followers into demanding an electoral reform to enable them to carry the electorate 'without benefit of Dev'. Further, the weapon of a referendum, though 'eminently constitutional', might be 'a dangerous precedent', and the *Irish Times* concluded by hoping that Fianna Fáil would reconsider the matter although 'as everybody knows', de Valera had been emitting 'veiled threats against PR' for many years back, especially during election campaigns when the odds were even. (Whenever this had happened, the *Irish Times* had taken him to task severely, and indicated that it was ready to do battle if de Valera should progress from intention to action.)[4]

It might have been expected that the surmises and inaccuracies in the *Irish Times'* leading article would be speedily pointed out in the columns of the government daily, the *Irish Press*. In the first place, de Valera's 1957 parliamentary majority, which was proportionately lower than the Conservative majority in Britain, was the first that any Irish party had secured since 1948, while Britain had not experienced a minority government since 1931. Then the accident that in 1958, as in 1922, there were just four significant parties, could not obscure the fact that in the intervening years others had emerged to prevent the formation of stable single-party governments. The story that the back-benchers of Fianna Fáil, realising that their aged leader could scarcely fight another election, were forcing his hand, seems pure surmise, and though it was often repeated by the *Irish Times* during the campaign, no evidence was ever adduced in its favour.

It was characteristic that when, at a press conference on 8 September, de Valera made his first official pronouncement that the abolition of PR was 'under consideration', he added that, in spite of some 'informal discussion' in the Fianna Fáil party and between the members of the government, fuller consideration was necessary. This news was headlined 'No definite decision yet' on the front page of the *Irish Press*.[5]

Both the *Irish Times* and the *Irish Independent* were highly amused at the suggestion that anyone in Fianna Fáil would have to be persuaded on a matter on which 'the Chief' had already made up his mind, but unless the press conference be dismissed as a subterfuge it is possible to infer that some of the deputies elected in 1957 on the lower preferences of others had expressed a natural fear that the change, while helping the party's future as a whole, might imperil theirs.[6] The rather pointed silence of the *Irish Press* shows that the party line was not laid down all at once, and, in any case, tends to refute rather than confirm the hypothesis that the back-benchers were forcing an unwilling de Valera to change the electoral system to their advantage.

True to its traditional policy of caution, the first editorial reaction of the *Independent* had been guarded. It merely disputed the expediency of a referendum on PR on the ground of expense and the presumption of a general satisfaction with the system among public men (in spite of what its own political correspondent had written on 28 August), and said that many people would doubt the wisdom of abolishing PR. By the time of de Valera's press conference the attitude had hardened and the *Independent* stood four-square on the necessity of 'representation for minorities', adducing the same arguments against change as the *Irish Times*.

Whatever doubtings and questionings may have gone on in Fianna Fáil were, however, settled by the time of the Ard Fheis (annual conference) on 28 October. Delegate after delegate (with none dissenting) spoke against the instability and weakness of PR governments and de Valera's final address was greeted with prolonged applause. He said that while he fully understood the case to be made for PR he would be failing in his duty if he neglected to put the issue to the people, when he had a sufficient Dáil majority to do so. The people must be the ultimate arbiters and the matter was sufficiently urgent to seek their opinion at once.[7] The party line was now quite clear.

Although both the original announcement in August and the press conference in September occurred during the parliamentary recess, that scarcely explains the slowness of the opposition's reaction. Only the Labour Party was immediately hostile. Fine Gael appears to have done a good deal of heart-searching before an official party policy was decided upon. This is not surprising in view of its ambivalent history on PR. The possibility that an electoral reform would ultimately help the party to become the only alternative government, instead of the leading partner in coalitions, must have occurred to the Fine Gael deputies. The *Independent* had hinted in August that it was not only in the government ranks that opponents of PR might be found. If this was so, it is a reasonable assumption that they were in Fine Gael, since Labour and Clann na Talmhan had nothing to gain and everything to lose by a reversion to the majority system, unless the former were imaginative enough to try to jostle Fine Gael out of the way and become the only alternative to Fianna Fáil—a not very likely development at that time.

When the news of the government's proposal appeared there were three possible courses open to Fine Gael: (1) to accept the bill in principle (or offer a token resistance); (2) to try to reach a compromise on the single transferable vote in single-member constituencies; (3) to offer all-out opposition together with Labour and the smaller parties and Independents. If Fine Gael were to collaborate with Fianna Fáil in passing the bill (or at least not to impede it), and so leave the way open for the people to judge, it could not have been accused of a dereliction of duty since the ultimate decision would not be for parliament to make. It could quite consistently allow the bill through and then campaign in the country against the changing of the electoral system.

As to the second option, it was mentioned many times during the debates, but there is no evidence that Fine Gael (or Labour) ever seriously pressed the matter, even when the debates were going against Fianna Fáil.[8]

The third course of vehement and uncompromising opposition to the bill both as a piece of legislation and as a subject for a referendum was eventually decided on by Fine Gael, as was made clear in a speech by Costello on 1 October.[9] The methods used to this end will be discussed below. The party front bench wholeheartedly entered into the fray, with the solitary exception of Liam Cosgrave, son of W. T. Cosgrave and a former Minister for External Affairs (1954-7), who made no speech whatever either in the Dáil or in the country during the campaign; and it was known that he was opposed to PR.

What was perhaps the determining factor in Fine Gael's attitude was the fear that the *first* election after the change would result in a widespread loss of seats, and thus of prestige, such as the party had experienced between 1932 and 1948 and did not wish to repeat, even though in the long run it might become the only practicable alternative to Fianna Fáil. This view was put forcefully in a leading article in the party monthly, the *National Observer,* some months after the debate began. It suggests that a long sojourn in the wilderness had implanted some of the 'small party' mentality in Fine Gael.[10]

The Dáil reassembled on 29 October and the government chief whip announced that the bill would shortly be introduced.[11] Apart from the newspapers and the parties, an early hostile reaction came from the Workers' Union of Ireland and the Dublin Corporation, which had an anti-Fianna Fáil majority.

The Third Amendment to the Constitution Bill was introduced by the Taoiseach on 12 November 1958. The debate between that day and 28 January 1959, when it was deemed to have been passed by the lower house, runs to 600,000 words in the official report.[12] To analyse these speeches comprehensively would go far beyond the scope of this work; it would also be a singularly unrewarding task, since most of the speeches were dull, unimaginative, not always precise in their references to foreign electoral experience, and, at times, dubious even in their analogies from Irish history. Both sides of the Dáil are impartially embraced in this criticism and even the front benches are not left out. A very few deputies made speeches of any value: for the government de Valera, Frank Aiken, Sean MacEntee, Erskine Childers, Sean Lemass (who spoke seldom), and a back-bencher Lionel Booth; for the opposition, John A. Costello and his son Declan, T. F. O'Higgins, Patrick McGilligan (Fine Gael) and Brendan Corish (Labour) and two Independent deputies, W. A. Sheldon and G. E. Russell. From the start it was clear that Fianna Fáil was faced with a double task: the tactical one of getting the bill through the Dáil and Senate as quickly as possible, and the strategic one of persuading the electorate. From both points of view the handling of the bill in its early stages in the Dáil would be important.

On the first reading (12 November) de Valera merely outlined the provisions of the bill: the expected abolition of the single transferable vote and the multi-number constituency and the introduction of the single non-transferable vote, and (to allay suspicions that the new constituencies would be 'rigged') a permanent commission under the chairmanship of a Supreme Court judge and consisting of six deputies, three from each side of the Dáil. According to normal practice, measures introduced by the government are not discussed on the first reading, but both Costello and Norton, the Labour leader, made use of the opportunity to anticipate their second reading speeches, to the great indignation of several ministers who protested that the rules of the House prevented them from replying.[13]

The second reading debate which lasted from 26 November until 16 December—the eve of the Christmas recess—in its early stages revealed the government and opposition cases in all their complexity. De Valera stated his case first: that the purpose of an election, to choose a government for five years, had at least since 1948 been frustrated by post-election bargaining, in which the people obviously could not have a say.[14] He went on to anticipate opposition criticisms—the timing of the bill was conditioned by the termination of the current twelve-year revision; foreign experience had shown that while PR had a disintegrating effect the majority system acted as an integrating agency. He added (to forestall charges of aiming at perpetual Fianna Fáil rule): 'Fianna Fáil knows that as a result of the passing of this bill an opposition will be built up which would almost certainly replace the existing government as an alternative government.' To the obvious question why he had not changed the system in 1937, de Valera replied that he had been anxious to keep, if possible, the system with which the people were familiar, and up to that time the predominance of certain issues had kept the number of parties down. Now, however, it could be seen that Irish PR made for a multiplicity of parties.

It was conceded by the *Irish Times* that de Valera had made the 'very best of a bad case'.[15] His speech was lucid and well-arranged, although, since he was nearly totally blind, he had to give it without notes. The one weakness lay in the unconvincing reason given for keeping the system in the 1937 Constitution; it is far more likely that the real reason was a purely tactical one. The arguments from foreign experience were apt. Apart from all value judgments PR has, in fact, acted as a disintegrating force and the majority system as an integrating one.[16] If the prime purpose of an election be the formation of a government through popular choice, the element of popular approval tends to be minimised whenever the parties fight independently and make post-election bargains, as had happened in Ireland since 1948. Again, since the constitutional procedure would prevent a direct appeal to the people without prior approval by the legislature, only a party with a stable majority could bring this off; a coalition or a single-party minority government would be most unlikely to get such a bill through the Dáil.

Fine Gael's attitude to the bill was summarised in an amendment tabled by Costello and Mulcahy on 26 November. The amendment listed the following arguments against abolishing PR and the probable consequences:

1. It would interfere with the legitimate rights of minorities;
2. it would be contrary to 'our democratic traditions';
3. it would lead to 'unrepresentative parliaments and arrogant government';

4. it would make the ending of Partition more difficult;
5. it had not been demanded by public opinion, and,
6. 'therefore, in present world conditions and in our economic circumstances [it] will impair rather than assist the solution of our national problems'.

The amendment would have refused the bill a second reading, and suggested in its place that a commission of experts be set up to examine and report on the existing system.[17]

The speeches of the Fine Gael leaders were as a rule heavily loaded on the side of prophecy: the government was taking a step of the utmost gravity and no one could predict the long-term effects on the party structure, although in the immediate future there would be an obvious advantage to Fianna Fáil. Costello seemed to take for granted a new alignment of political forces with the passing of the Treaty generation: 'We are coming to the end of an era. We do not know how Parties may split up . . . There may very well be what I might describe, with not any over-emphasis, as a Radical Party. Certainly, in a few years there will be a break-up of the present political Parties. God alone knows what will be the result.'[18]

This was the most telling opposition argument: that at a transitional period when the Treaty generation was about to pass out of active politics (by the next election all those who fought between 1916 and 1921 would be at least sixty), de Valera was seeking to force the parties into a mould of his own choosing to prevent a more 'rational' alignment. Fears were also expressed that the Northern Unionists (although they would have done better under the plurality system than under PR) would be less likely to be coaxed into a United Ireland if PR were abolished; that the subversive groups which had secured the election of four deputies to the existing Dáil would be forced underground, and that Protestants would have a smaller chance of getting into the Dáil.

While the defenders of PR spent a good deal of time and energy in refuting the charges made by the government, one is inclined to conclude from the casual manner in which these issues were handled that at heart speakers from the opposition believed that Irish conditions are somehow unique, and the prevailing sentiment (dressed up in a typically rhetorical style) may well have been James Dillon's:

This is not the United States of America. This is not Great Britain. Harold Macmillan has not fought Hugh Gaitskell in a civil war. Nobody looks across the floor of an English Parliament to recall that his father may have fallen at the hands of another member's father . . .

I know that, happily, the bitternesses of the past are receding behind us but I shall obey no injunction to forget the past or those who have gone before. I think we should remember all of them but forget the injuries in so far as we can. But make no demand upon us to act like Englishmen or to act like the polyglot people of the United States of

America, for we are neither one nor the other. We are a cohesive, perhaps too intimate, people, knowing the history of our father and our father's father. We are as God made us and as history has destined us to be.[19]

So far as the charge was concerned, that the first-past-the-post system would prove detrimental to religious minorities, one of the few Protestants in the Dáil, Lionel Booth, answered:

> At present, there are only four Protestant TDs. One of these only [Deputy Sheldon of Donegal] lays claim to election by Protestants, and he has already spoken and voted in favour of the institution of majority voting instead of PR. The other three are all party members who stood as party candidates and in none of their constituencies are there enough Protestant voters to give the quota which is necessary to secure election under PR.[20]

And so the second reading debate dragged on until it degenerated into an examination of the previous thirty-five years. Speeches of de Valera for PR and by Costello and Dillon against, were resurrected and triumphantly brandished by the other side as proofs of inconsistency. In winding up the debate on 16 December de Valera produced a photostat copy of the Cumann na nGaedheal advertisement of 1927 (referred to above),[21] went through it point by point and, claiming that it made a better case against PR than he could make, presented it to Costello across the floor of the House.[22] The second reading passed by seventy-six votes to fifty-eight; two Independents, Russell and Sheldon, voting for the bill together with Fianna Fáil, and the rest of the House voted against.

With the passing of the second reading the principle of the bill had been approved by the Dáil, and since there were not many details, it might have been expected that the committee stage would not last long. Fianna Fáil therefore seemed to be winning the tactical battle without much difficulty; and as far as the strategic one was concerned, by the beginning of December the *Irish Times* was gloomily assuming that PR would be lost 'if only because the Fianna Fáil Party's machine is more efficient'.[23]

A newcomer, however, to the campaign was Miss Enid Lakeman, research secretary of the Proportional Representation Society, who gave a series of lectures in December strongly urging the people not to desert the cause of 'electoral justice', and between then and the referendum she bombarded the Irish newspapers with letters on every aspect of the system. Like her predecessor, J. H. Humphreys, Miss Lakeman is an able publicist, and she skilfully marshalled all the evidence in her favour.

Miss Lakeman's campaign was the first evidence of public interest in the electoral problem. At the same time, various debating societies in Dublin and Cork held several meetings at which politicians of both sides were invited to state their case. Their example was followed by the rural debating societies, mainly under the auspices of Macra na Feirme (children of the farm), an organisation established to raise the intellectual and cultural level of the farming community. Common to all these societies was an attitude of earnest inquiry in the midst of perplexity. The problem seemed so complicated, the arguments for and against so difficult to evaluate, and the Dáil speeches so unenlightening that they had to provide an open forum for the more articulate politicians; Lionel Booth and Declan Costello were among the most frequently invited. Academic experts called in were either members of the PR Society or in some way favourable to the system. From the beginning every medium of public opinion, apart from the Fianna Fáil journals, seemed against the government.[24]

The tactical battle was renewed on 8 January 1959, when the committee stage of the bill was initiated. In the meantime one new and very important factor had arisen—a report (at first unconfirmed) on 8 January that de Valera would be nominated by his party for the presidential election which would occur in June.[25] Already Fine Gael had selected its candidate, General Sean MacEoin, a hero of the War of Independence, who had not only held office in both Coalitions but had set his heart on the presidency since 1938. The office of Head of the State is naturally above politics and the first election had been averted by both Fianna Fáil and Fine Gael agreeing on the personality of Dr Douglas Hyde, the leading figure in the Irish language revival movement. In 1945 there was a straightforward party contest, Sean T. O'Kelly, Tanaiste (deputy Prime Minister) to de Valera, beating General MacEoin and another opponent by a large majority. In 1952 O'Kelly was returned unopposed, but the Constitution forbade more than two terms.

Why did de Valera decide at this time to leave the political arena? As yet there is little evidence to go on. The political correspondent of the *Irish Times*, writing with the gift of hindsight, said that de Valera had made it clear to his close associates some time in 1958 that he would not contest another general election. His increasing blindness and age (he was then in his seventy-seventh year) may well have combined to make him seek a less disputatious role.[26]

Whatever the motive, however, de Valera's decision was grist to the opposition's mill. They were able to claim that Fianna Fáil was throwing the personality of the leader into the scales against PR, that an emotional appeal would be made to the people not to refuse 'Dev's last request', and they furiously denounced any suggestion to hold both elections on the same day as an attempt to defraud the people.

The opposition resumed the tactical engagement by scoring heavily against Neil Blaney, the Minister for Local Government, when he introduced, on 8 January, a technical bill to provide a suitable ballot paper for use at a referendum: Fine Gael was able to claim that existing law prescribed that the ballot contain an intelligible résumé of the question at issue for the voter's benefit, while Blaney's bill would merely list the short title, 'The Third Amendment to the Constitution Bill, 1959'.[27]

Another tactical setback occurred on the opening day in committee (8 January). The referendum bill was drawn up in a curious form, the three main provisions—abolition of STV, the substitution of the single-seat constituency, and the constituency commission—all being relegated to a schedule, while the bill proper merely prescribed that the Constitution be amended in accordance with the schedule. At the beginning of the debate the Ceann Comhairle ruled that the schedule must be discussed as a whole 'to avoid duplication of debate'. The opposition parties hotly objected that this would limit their natural right of discussion. When a long procedural wrangle culminated in Mulcahy's being ordered out of the House by the Leas Ceann Comhairle (Deputy Speaker) and he refused to go, de Valera intervened to say that he had no wish to restrict full discussion of the bill. Finally, an arrangement was reached by which the three sections of the schedule were discussed separately, as well as the bill.[28]

Fine Gael and Labour were now free to air the same views as on the second reading, and they did so, especially in the days immediately after the agreement. Not only were second-reading speeches rehashed, but matters of little relevance were dragged into the discussion on the schedules. Section I dealt with single-seat constituencies only, but many speeches on 14 January dealt with the case for and against coalitions and the hypothesis that, in the future, Labour would be more likely to join with Fianna Fáil than Fine Gael. Fianna Fáil back-benchers complained that the opposition was trying to prolong the debate interminably, but there was little they could do to stop them. Every argument produced a counter-argument. As an Independent deputy said on 20 January: 'The longer this debate continues the more we go around in circles, and the more the people of the country are confused to know what it is all about'.[29]

When the section dealing with the abolition of the multi-seat constituency had been passed, James Dillon pleaded that the single transferable vote be kept, and said that his party would be willing to accept that arrangement, not as a second best but as 'second worst'. No willingness to compromise was shown by Fianna Fáil, but at the same time no other opposition speaker supported Dillon's offer. The last section dealing with a constituency commission was derided by Fine Gael as impracticable and aimed at giving 'a thin veneer of respectability to an unscrupulous political manoeuvre'.[30]

The final stage was reached on 28 January. Costello adverted to de Valera's running for the presidency and to the fears that he would try to draw the office of President more closely to the government. Costello repeated his argument that a dying generation had no right to impose its will on the young, and made the point that, if the bill were passed, it would need something like a revolution to change the new system. Winding up the debate, de Valera claimed that it was not undemocratic to make the people the final arbiters of an issue on which the legislature was irreconcilably split.[31]

The stable Fianna Fáil majority carried the bill through the Dáil. It then had to go before the Senate.[32] The members of the Irish Senate are partly elected by the Dáil deputies and partly by various local authorities, but as a rule the Senate reproduces the political alignments of the Dáil. The legislative power of the Senate does not extend beyond a ninety-day moratorium on bills passed by the Dáil—compared with one year in the case of the British House of Lords. Since the establishment of the Senate under the 1937 Constitution, no bill introduced by a government had been defeated. Although the original intention to create a vocational Second Chamber was largely frustrated by the habit of electing politicians who could not get into (or stay in) the Dáil, there is one small but influential group unaffected by the ordinary political currents—the six senators who represent the National University of Ireland and Trinity College, Dublin. The first three are generally Catholics and the last three Protestant (until the 1960s) and over the years they built up a reputation for a sophisticated approach to politics.

None of them, however, had engaged in original research on electoral systems,[33] and, as a result, they had to base their views on the material as presented to them in the debate, which meant that the larger volume of the pro-PR publications produced its inevitable effect. Their views were, however, forcefully expressed and were not unrelated to the fact that, in the final stage, on 19 March, the Senate threw out the bill by a majority of twenty-nine votes to twenty-eight, out of a total membership of sixty. Two of the three absent (through illness) were supporters of the government. The anti-Fianna Fáil press at once exulted in the defeat: 'a very unpleasant set-back',[34] the political correspondent of the *Irish Independent* pronounced, although his editor, true to his usual form, refrained from producing a leading article on it.

During the debates in the Senate the university senators (especially Professor Quinlan) had urged the government to shelve the bill until a commission of experts had examined and reported on the system. They now took advantage of the government's tactical defeat and asked the voters to keep 'our distinctive Irish form of Proportional Representation' until such a commission had been set up and had performed its task.[35]

To clinch this argument the university senators called on the leaders of the opposition parties to promise that, if successful, they would appoint an expert commission, and that they would implement any changes recommended by the commission by means of a 'fairly-worded' referendum allowing the people to judge each major recommendation separately.[36]

On 5 May, the debate on the government motion to pass the unaltered bill over the veto of the Senate opened in the Dáil. Fine Gael and Labour demanded that, in view of 'widespread opposition', the bill be withdrawn and a commission appointed instead, and for five days the House was treated to the regurgitated speeches of the previous December. The fact that the result was a foregone conclusion may have accounted for the small attendance and lack of public interest in the last stages of the debate. On 13 May the government motion passed by seventy-five votes to fifty-six.

The government had now attained its tactical objective, but at a greater cost in time and effort than it had expected. The strategic objective had to be reached in a four-week campaign, since the time of the presidential election was constitutionally determined and could not fall later than 18 June. Clearly the decision to hold election and referendum on the same day was intended to utilise the candidature of de Valera in the former to help his party in the latter—'an endless pity', the *Irish Times* called it, and asserted that although de Valera was certain to win the office to which his standing in the country entitled him, nevertheless, 'the laurels will be just a little tarnished'.[37] The excuse which de Valera gave on 8 April that 'public convenience would be best met' by having the two on the same day was unconvincing. Although the presidential election could not be postponed, there was no technical reason why the referendum should be held on the same day.

The campaign in the country, which had been going on intermittently since Christmas, now was intensified. At first there was little evidence of public reaction. Two weeks after the Senate defeat the *Irish Times* wrote that there was no knowing how the referendum would go, since the issue was not one about which the average elector was much concerned. Still, it soon became obvious that the propaganda for PR was much more effective than that against. The organisational nucleus provided by the Proportional Representation Society and its Irish friends became the basis of concerted efforts. There never was a pamphlet stating the case against PR. Printed information issuing from the pro-PR side had always been ample, and there was an addition: the reprint of a series of articles by Proinsias Mac Aonghusa published in the *Irish Times,* mainly historical, but with a strong pro-PR bias, and written with the skill of the experienced journalist.[38]

Much more serious was a comparative study of the merits of electoral systems produced by the *Tuarim* research group entitled 'PR—For or against'. The authors, a group of very competent young men, were sincerely anxious to be objective. Still, the influence of the pro-PR literature is clearly evident, in particular in the evaluation of foreign experience. In its discussion of the concrete Irish aspects of the matter, the pamphlet is both careful and informative. Its conclusions were nonetheless clear for being tentatively stated: if the system had to be changed, 'the best possible alternative' ought to be presented, and the government should wait until an independent commission had found this alternative.[39] It is not unlikely that, had de Valera been willing to compromise to the extent of permitting the alternative vote, this group would have reached different conclusions.

Against this volume of hostile opinion the government mustered all its resources: daily articles in the *Irish Press,* leaflets, posters, and broadsheets on the advantages of the first-past-the-post system, in particular its simplicity and directness. Meetings were organised by the local associations in every constituency. They were vigorously supported by the Cumann na nGaedheal ex-Minister, Ernest Blythe, who made no secret of his preference for stable government at the cost of 'fair representation', and the Independent (Protestant) deputy, W. A. Sheldon,[40] who was allocated one of the six party broadcasts from Radio Eireann, with the intention of counteracting the impression that all Southern Protestants were as attached as Canon Luce to PR.

Fine Gael was greatly encouraged by the attempted mobilisation of public opinion against the government—the *National Observer* had predicted in March that the defeat of the bill in the Senate, and especially the vigour of the academic opposition, would turn the scales against Fianna Fáil. But Fine Gael also had to run a presidential campaign for General MacEoin, which it scarely could have hoped would be successful, and the Fine Gael front-benchers divided their speeches between encomiums of their candidate and of the existing electoral system, while Fianna Fáil speakers took 'Dev's' election for granted. The government became increasingly sensitive to gibes about the causal connection between de Valera's candidature and the abolition of PR. Towards the end of May, when it was discovered that under the existing law General MacEoin was liable to postage expenses for his thousands of election addresses, the government hastily introduced a bill to allow him to send them post free.[41]

It might have been thought at the end of May that no further argument could possibly be adduced on one side or the other, and that the campaign would run down in the last two weeks. But yet another initiative was to come; the Irish Congress of Trade Unions announced in the first week of June that its 500,000 members were unequivocally for PR and that it was setting up a special PR committee to mobilise uncommitted opinion before the referendum. The chairman of the committee asserted that he was not acting on behalf of the Labour Party (which, as usual, campaigned sporadically) but in the general interest of the 'democratic system of election' as against 'dictatorial jobbery'. The ICTU campaign was especially strong in Dublin and the other cities; as polling day drew near they appealed for cars to take voters to the polls.[42]

At the very end of the campaign, although the issue was always doubtful, the chances of the opposition seemed a good deal better than in the previous December, and the feeling that Fianna Fáil was having the worst of the argument was increasing. In December the *Irish Times* (although its hostility to the bill never wavered) was pessimistically assuming that the superior party machine would win.[43] At the end of the Senate debate it confessed itself unable to predict the result. By the middle of May its outlook was more cheerful: 'It is conceivable, indeed . . . that the intelligent few . . . will swing the balance' (15 May). On polling day (17 June) the *Irish Times* produced a leading article that frankly directed 'the intelligent few' on how to vote—it even reproduced a facsimile of the ballot paper with a cross opposite the 'no' column.

On the evening of polling day, with a nice sense of timing, de Valera resigned his office as Taoiseach at the end of forty-two years in politics. With an equal sense of propriety he never made a comment on the referendum result.

The result showed a turnout of 58.3 per cent, higher than expected but still lower than at a general election; it was the first time that less than a million votes were polled in a national election. De Valera won the presidency by a majority (56.33 per cent) that was comfortable but not overwhelming, and MacEoin polled better than in 1945. On the other hand the government lost the referendum by 48.22 per cent to 51.78 per cent. There were 486,989 votes cast for the retention of PR and 453,322 against.[44]

In spite of all the publicity given to the referendum, the poll in the presidential election was very slightly higher (0.01 per cent). In the presidential election de Valera won in thirty-four constituencies, MacEoin in six—one Cork constituency, four in Dublin and his own division, Longford-Westmeath. In the referendum there was a majority of 'yes' votes in nineteen, and of 'no' votes in twenty-one constituencies.

If we compare the constituency breakdown of the Fianna Fáil vote in the 1957 general election with the 'yes' vote in the referendum, there was a national swing of only 0.08 per cent away from the government, and it was far from uniform. The greatest swing took place in the seven Dublin constituencies and in one of the five Cork constituencies. In most of the rural areas there was a swing *towards* the government, which was highest in eight constituencies where in 1957 Fianna Fáil did not secure 50 per cent of the vote. These eight were scattered throughout the country. In 1957 the party secured a majority in thirteen constituencies, all rural except one in Dublin; in 1959 they won in nineteen constituencies, including eight of the former.[45]

To sum up, the government lost the referendum by a margin of just above 3.5 per cent in a national turnout of just over half the registered votes. Clearly the referendum was lost in the cities of Dublin and Cork. The pro-PR majority in Dublin alone, where the trade unions were strong, sufficed to turn the tide. The *Irish Review and Annual* for 1959, published by the *Irish Times,* wrote: 'The effect of the trades' unions' intervention may have been seen in Dublin, the hard core of resistance to the proposed change in the electoral system ... the solid majority of 45,762 in Dublin City and County had tipped a balance of 12,130 *against* it in the remainder of the country.'[46]

7

The Two-and-a-half Party System, 1961-77

I
THE GENERAL ELECTIONS OF 1961 AND 1965

The years 1959 to 1961 marked a watershed in Irish political development. Each of the three main parties elected a new leader and the long ascendancy of the Treaty generation was plainly coming to an end.

De Valera's successor in Fianna Fáil was Sean Lemass, who since 1945, when he was appointed Tanaiste (deputy Prime Minister), had been the obvious heir-apparent. Although Lemass had fought in Easter week (at the age of seventeen), his political career did not begin until his election for a Dublin constituency in 1924. He had been appointed Minister for Industry and Commerce in 1932 and had held the same portfolio through every Fianna Fáil administration since. (During the war years he also served as Minister for Supplies). A pragmatic, hard-headed politician, Lemass in one of his first speeches as Taoiseach served notice that he would not indulge in the usual threadbare platitudes about Partition, and also hinted that it was time to bury the civil war animosities. In his last administration de Valera had elevated to ministerial rank a number of young politicians who had entered the Dáil in 1948 or later—Jack Lynch, Neil Blaney, and Kevin Boland. Lemass was to continue this trend with Dr. P. J. Hillery (1959) and Charles Haughey (1961). Although he never strove to emulate the charismatic appeal of 'the Chief', Lemass was, in the opinion of one authority, a better chairman in Cabinet.[1]

In October 1959 General Mulcahy resigned as leader of Fine Gael, and at the same time John A. Costello resigned as leader of the opposition; so the curious dual leadership which had persisted in Fine Gael since 1948 came to an end. Mulcahy's retirement was in its own way as significant as de Valera's. He had been Minister for Defence in the first two Dáils and Chief of Staff of the Republican Army until 1922; after Collins' assassination he was a possible rival to Cosgrave for the leadership of the Free State government.[2] Unlike that of Fianna Fáil, the leadership of Fine Gael was contested, by James Dillon and Liam Cosgrave, and Dillon won, in a vote of all the party members of both Houses, by an undisclosed majority. On becoming leader of Fine Gael he automatically became leader of the opposition.

Although considerably younger than their predecessors the new leaders of the biggest parties were mature politicians with longer experience than most European party leaders could boast at that time. The new leader of the Labour Party was much their junior both in years and experience. In 1960 William Norton resigned the leadership after twenty-eight years in office. Although born in 1900, and thus of the same generation as Lemass and Dillon, Norton's health was then poor, and it was noted that in the 1957 election he did not campaign outside his own constituency, Kildare.[3] The obvious successor was Brendan Corish, who had been elected for Wexford in 1945 on the death of his father, who had represented the constituency since 1921. (This, incidentally, was one of only two by-elections which Fianna Fáil did not win between 1935 and 1947.) He was appointed to a parliamentary secretaryship in 1948, at the age of thirty, and held a Cabinet post in the second Coalition. On his election, Corish confirmed that under his leadership the Labour Party would steer clear of future coalitions, as had been decided after the electoral debacle of 1957, at the annual party conference of that year, held in Cork.

The most important events of the first Lemass government were a remarkable economic recovery and Ireland's emergence, after decades of isolation, into international politics.

1. The first Programme for Economic Expansion, approved by the government in November 1958, was drawn up by the Secretary of the Department of Finance, Mr T. K. Whitaker, who ascribed his departure from his usual bureaucratic task of controlling public expenditure to the need to combat 'the all too prevalent mood of despondency about the country's future'.[4] (The causes were the exhaustion of the assets accumulated during the war, an annual growth rate of 2 per cent, 'perceptibly slower . . . than the British and quite markedly slower than those prevailing in the OEEC countries;'[5] and an annual emigration rate of 14.8 per 1000.) The Whitaker Plan involved a massive injection of state capital into productive enterprises over a five-year period, and also greatly stimulated the private sector in industry. The programme succeeded beyond its author's expectations. By the end of the five years 1959-63 the growth rate had increased to 4 per cent, investment had doubled and emigration was down to 5.7 per 1000. Although the Whitaker Plan had been prepared under de Valera, its implementation fell almost entirely within Lemass's premiership.

2. The other feature was perhaps more unexpected. Until the admission of the Republic to the United Nations (December 1955) Irish participation in international bodies—especially the Council of Europe—had been virtually confined to lamentations about the iniquity of Partition.[6] In the late fifties, however, Frank Aiken, Minister for External Affairs, took an independent stance on international issues in his speeches at the UN. In 1960 a member of the Irish delegation to the UN, Dr Conor Cruise O'Brien, was

appointed UN Commissioner in Katanga and in 1961 Irish troops were sent abroad for the first time, as part of the UN peace-keeping force in the Congo—a decision which was taken by Lemass in spite of objections by senior members of his Cabinet.[7]

Lastly, in July 1961, following the decision by the Macmillan government to apply for British membership of the European Community, the Irish government also applied for membership, Lemass justifying the step as a consequence of the extremely close trading relationships between the two countries.

The arrangements for the referendum on PR took up most of the government's time during the spring and summer of 1959. Having lost the referendum, they were obliged to rush through the Dáil a new measure revising the constituencies, since the twelve-year limit permitted by the Constitution had been reached. The number of five-seat and four-seat constituencies was left unchanged and the number of three-seat divisions was reduced from twenty-two to twenty-one, leaving a Dáil of 144 instead of 147 deputies.[8] But the bill never became law, because it was successfully challenged in the High Court by Dr. John O'Donovan (then a Fine Gael Senator; formerly a parliamentary secretary who had lost his seat in 1957). The points at issue were three sub-sections of Article 16 of the Constitution, which specified that the total number of deputies should not exceed one per 20,000 (16.2.2); that 'so far as it is practicable' the ratio of deputies to population should be uniform throughout the country (16.2.3), and that the revisions, which should occur at least once in twelve years, should pay due regard to changes in population distribution, as ascertained at the previous census (16.2.4).

In the government bill the national average was one deputy to 20,100, but there were considerable variations. In the four western counties of Donegal, Galway, Mayo and Kerry, whose population had been continuously declining, the ratio was one deputy to 17,758; in Dublin city it was one to 22,753.

When the case was presented in the High Court, the Attorney General argued that hitherto, outside the cities and county boroughs, constituencies had been based on the administrative counties, which were natural communities, and that this justified over-representing the western counties. However, in his judgment Mr Justice Budd ruled that 'there is nothing in the Constitution about constituencies being based on counties', and that the variations in the 1959 bill contravened Article 16.2.3.[9]

The High Court decision in *O'Donovan v. the Attorney General* was not given until 1961, and it was quickly followed by another Electoral (Amendment) Bill, introduced by the Minister for Local Government, Neil Blaney. Only three constituencies (all five-seaters) had their boundaries unchanged, as compared with the 1947 Act. The number of five-seat constituencies remained at nine, but there were adjustments between the three and four-seat divisions. The total number of deputies was reduced from 147 to 144.

Since Mr Justice Budd, while rejecting the 1959 scheme, did not specify the variation from the national average which would be tolerable (the so-called 'tolerance limits')—except to imply that a deviation of 1,000 on either side of the national average would be permissible—the government took the precaution of referring the 1961 bill to the Supreme Court for an advance opinion on its constitutionality. The Supreme Court agreed that absolute equality was unattainable, but also refused to provide a yardstick, merely indicating that they would decide if a scheme was *not* constitutional, but they implicitly agreed that a deviation of 1,000, such as occurred in some cases in the bill, would come within the scope of Article 16.2.3.[10] The bill accordingly became law.

The Sixteenth Dáil, elected in 1957, was the first since 1938 whose life was not terminated by a political crisis. A general election was not con-stitutionally due until March 1962, but in September 1961, during the summer recess, Lemass announced a dissolution with polling on 15 Octo-ber. The only excuse given for having an election then was that Ireland's application for membership of the EEC would involve 'delicate' negotia-tions and that it would be well to have the election out of the way first. The campaign, lasting a mere three weeks in unusually warm autumn weather, was the dullest on record.[11] All parties campaigned independently and no alternative to Fianna Fáil appeared in sight. Fine Gael appealed in its manifesto for 'a mandate from the people to form a Fine Gael govern-ment', arguing somewhat implausibly that 'in the new economic climate of the Common Market' Fine Gael could be trusted to maintain 'its good record in all the negotiations it has undertaken heretofore'[12]—the last was in 1931! Labour stressed its independence of all other parties, but none of its spokesmen could suggest what might happen if the election produced a deadlock.[13] Fianna Fáil campaigned on its record, especially on the Economic Programme, the fruits of which were already appearing.

Speaking tours by the leaders were considerably reduced in this cam-paign. Lemass addressed only fifteen meetings, and Dillon thirty-one.[14] The closing stages of the campaign were overshadowed by an unfounded rumour that Irish troops had been massacred in the Congo and some meet-ings were cancelled. But the final Fine Gael rally in Dublin was disrupted by hecklers from Irish language organisations, who were incensed by the Fine Gael pledge (the only original one in its manifesto) to abolish all com-pulsory Irish, both in the public service and as a school subject.

The results showed a fall in turnout since 1957. Fianna Fáil's share of the vote dropped by 4.5 per cent and it lost eight seats, Fine Gael increased from forty to forty-seven, and Labour from eleven to fifteen. But with a combined share of the first preferences equal to Fianna Fáil's, it was plain that Fine Gael and Labour were no longer helping each other in transfers and Fianna Fáil's 'bonus' of seats was the highest since 1943. The coalition mentality had all but disappeared.

Although it was not noted at the time, the most significant feature of the 1961 general election was a further evolution of the Irish party system. Since 1948 there had been two competitive groups jockeying for power, Fianna Fáil versus the Rest. But since the smaller parties were now virtually annihilated there was developing what could be called (as in West Germany) a 'two-and-a-half party' system, in which the third would trail far behind the second. In the election Clann na Talmhan was reduced from three deputies to two, the founders Donnellan and Blowick, and a mere 1.5 per cent of the national poll. Clann na Poblachta fared worse: it still had only one seat and MacBride failed once more to re-enter the Dáil; he had tried unsuccessfully in two Dublin by-elections since his defeat in 1957. Sinn Féin put up twenty candidates, but since they were committed to continuing the futile policy of abstention, all of them, including the four elected in 1957, were defeated. Lastly, a new party called the National Progressive Democrats, formed in 1958 by Dr Noel Browne and Jack McQuillan (also ex-Clann na Poblachta), with a vague left-wing programme, just secured the election of its two leaders. In 1963 the NPD deputies joined the Labour Party.

To avoid repetition, the demise of the two Clanns can be recounted here. Both maintained a notional existence until 1965. In 1964 Donnellan died and his son was elected in the ensuing by-election as a Fine Gael candidate. When the general election of 1965 took place, Blowick, the leader and last deputy of Clann na Talmhan, announced his retirement. No candidate came forward to contest his Mayo seat and the party faded from the scene. In the same election Clann na Poblachta fielded four candidates (MacBride, then Secretary General of the International Commission of Jurists, did not stand.) Its share of the national vote dropped to less than 1 per cent, and again only one candidate was elected, James Tully of Cavan. A few months later the party was formally wound up. (Tully sat on as an Independent deputy until 1969 when he too was defeated.) Thus ended two minor parties, one of which had survived longer than any minor group in the history of the state, while the other had achieved at its first electoral test the highest share of the vote ever secured by a minor party—pushing Labour into fourth place—but it had never recovered from the internal strife of 1951.[15]

Fianna Fáil was now two seats short of a majority, but with the support of two Independents Lemass carried on; he did not try to spring a snap election, as de Valera was accustomed to do. During the next four years economic growth continued, though at a slightly slower pace than during the first five-year plan.[16] De Gaulle's veto on the British application to join the EEC (January 1963) meant the consequential withdrawal of the Irish application, but this may well have been a blessing in disguise, since the Irish application had made singularly little progress during the previous year-and-a-half, and the EEC Commission had not issued an opinion as to whether the country was sufficiently advanced economically to shoulder the burdens of full Community membership.[17]

The electoral system attracted attention during these years. In a penetrating series of articles entitled 'What is wrong with the Dáil?', published in the *Irish Times* (19-22 August 1963), Dr David Thornley pointed to the difficulty of any party securing a majority of Dáil seats in the near future. He predicted that the country would be faced with three parties 'not differing decisively in size' and that in consequence Fianna Fáil would be compelled to abandon its 'majority bent' tradition; a Fianna Fáil/Labour coalition was, he suggested, the most logical outcome.[18]

In March 1965 Lemass announced a dissolution, this time eighteen months before it was constitutionally due. The pretext was a by-election loss in Mid-Cork. But it is more probable that the Taoiseach wished to capitalise on the popularity accruing from his completely unexpected visit to Belfast to meet the Northern Premier, Captain Terence O'Neill, in January of that year. That visit, the first ever official visit of a head of the government in Dublin to his counterpart in Belfast, merely produced a joint communiqué of unexceptionable generality and the promise of future contacts, including a return visit by O'Neill to Dublin. But the fury which it aroused among extreme Unionists—the Rev. Ian Paisley was then emerging as a formidable political figure—immediately redounded to the credit of both Lemass and O'Neill.[19]

In the election Fianna Fáil once more campaigned on its record of continuous, if somewhat slackened, economic growth; but the whole character of its electoral appeal had changed dramatically. To quote one observer, 'Since 1959 Mr Lemass has worked wonders with this material [his party]. He has cemented the loyalties while refurbishing the image. Thirty years ago this was a party of republicanism, language revival, economic protection; today it is a party of realism, talks with Captain O'Neill, growth, planning, free trade'.[20]

Wonders too had apparently been worked within Fine Gael. In May 1964 it had adopted an ambitious policy document entitled *The Just Society*, which Declan Costello, now a front-bencher, had produced singlehanded. This did not seriously challenge the industrial targets of the Second Economic Programme, but placed much greater emphasis on social welfare. Ireland, it pointed out, had a lower rate of expenditure on welfare than any EEC country, although its *per capita* income was about the same as the poorest, Italy. The Costello Plan called for much higher levels of social spending (welfare and education), a national incomes policy, and planning rather than programming.[21] With its adoption Fine Gael appeared to have made a spectacular move to the left of Fianna Fáil in respect of social policy.

Fine Gael's commitment to *The Just Society* was viewed at the time by Dr Garret FitzGerald (soon to begin his meteoric political career) as offering the party a better chance of a future coalition with Labour. In the earlier Coalitions he admitted that 'the papering over of wide policy differences between Fine Gael and its Left-wing partners led to weak governments, susceptible to pressures from too many different angles'.[22] However, Dr Fitz-Gerald's optimism was premature. During the campaign Fianna Fáil skilfully provoked Corish into a more definite avowal than in 1961 that he would not join in a coalition with either 'conservative' party but wait for the day when Labour would be in a position to implement its own policies.[23] The Labour manifesto, stressing the need for state control of economic activity and increased opportunities for employment, did not seem markedly different from Fine Gael's—if anything, it seemed more conservative.[24] (Incidentally, in 1965 Labour managed for the first time to field as candidates a number of professional men, including Dr John O'Donovan—a recent convert from Fine Gael—and Dr Noel Browne, but none was elected.)

The 1965 campaign was, perhaps, the first really 'modern' election in the Republic. Under the pragmatic leadership of Lemass relations between the two major parties had lost the bitterness of earlier years. Economic and social issues were debated in a more sophisticated manner; although, needless to say, party points were still scored, and many Fianna Fáil spokesmen questioned the enthusiasm of conservative-minded senior members of Fine Gael, like Dillon and Cosgrave, for the party's *appertura a sinistra*.

Another potent factor in political development was the national television service, Radio Telefís Eireann, which had been established in December 1961 as a state-sponsored body, like Radio Eireann, under the ultimate control of the Minister for Posts and Telegraphs. During the 1965 election, party political telecasts were watched by one-third of the population, a far higher proportion than listened to the radio broadcasts.[25] Also, and with far-reaching implications for the future, current affairs programmes on television were probing into controversial issues, discussion of which would have been unthinkable until then; for although Radio Eireann had been running programmes on current affairs for nearly twenty years it had always steered clear of controversial Irish issues and well merited the sardonic description 'a political eunuch'.[26] Side by side with this development, there appeared in the Dublin daily newspapers a new incisive type of editorial and political commentary, replacing the more anaemic style of earlier years.[27]

The election resulted in a higher turnout—1.253 million votes (74.5 per cent) as against 1.170 million (69.9 per cent) in 1961. The three main parties all increased their share of the poll, Fianna Fáil by 3.9 per cent, Fine Gael by 2.1 per cent and Labour by 3.8 per cent; but while Labour gained six seats and Fianna Fáil two, Fine Gael remained unchanged at forty-seven seats. These gains were secured at the expense of Independents and minor parties, who dropped to three seats and 2.8 per cent of the votes, the lowest ever.[28] Fianna Fáil's share of the poll increased in thirty-three out of thirty-eight constituencies. Fine Gael fluctuated more, being up in twenty-one constituencies and down in seventeen; but it plainly inherited many of the votes previously cast for Clann na Talmhan, since its greatest gains were in the two Mayo constituencies.

Another feature of the 1965 election worth mentioning was the final eclipse of the Treaty generation. Dr James Ryan, the Minister for Finance (who had sponsored the Whitaker Plan), announced his retirement from the Dáil at the outset of the campaign, and after the election the outgoing Tanaiste, Sean McEntee, was relegated to the back benches, leaving Lemass and Frank Aiken as the only survivors of the first Fianna Fáil government still in office; while Patrick McGilligan, the last survivor in the Dáil of Cosgrave's governments, lost his seat for Dublin North-Central.

II

THE 1968 REFERENDUM ON PR AND THE GENERAL ELECTION OF 1969

'The only political reputation I have is as an expert constituency reviser'.
Mr Kevin Boland (*Hibernia,* 22 July 1977, 9.)

(a) In the election of 1965 Lemass had won an overall majority. Moreover he had improved his party's performance in terms of seats after three *regular* general elections, a feat never achieved by his famous leader. Nevertheless, the margin was the narrowest possible—one seat; and in his first speech after the results were declared the Taoiseach hinted that the electoral system might have to be re-examined: 'There are probably many methods of reducing the disadvantages of the present system of electing Dáil deputies other than those put forward in 1959, and there is an obligation on all of us to do some thinking about them.'[29] In two articles written shortly afterwards, Dr Garret FitzGerald agreed that in the foreseeable future the existing three-party system was unlikely to yield either adequate majorities or coherent oppositions. He made a strong case for the single transferable vote in single-member constituencies, pointing out that it had been proposed by Fine Gael in 1959, and that its use in by-elections gave it the merit of familiarity.[30] This indicated that when next the electoral system was in question there might be sufficient support from Fine Gael for a compromise with Fianna Fáil—particularly since the new leader, Cosgrave, was known to be less than enthusiastic about PR. (A few weeks after the articles appeared FitzGerald was elected as a Senator in the Fine Gael interest.)

The opportunity did not occur for nearly three years. The rest of 1965 and 1966 were uneventful, marked by steady economic expansion and a substantial slowing down of emigration. In November 1966 there was a change in the leadership of the government when Lemass resigned, for health reasons. He had already indicated his intention to do so and when the resignation finally came two factions were lined up in support of the candidatures of Charles J. Haughey, Minister for Agriculture (first elected to the Dáil in 1957) and George Colley, Minister for Industry and Commerce (first elected in 1961), for the leadership of Fianna Fáil. Both were representative of the 'new blood' which Lemass had introduced into the government during his term of office, but neither had anything approaching majority support among the deputies. With the appearance of a third candidate, Neil Blaney, Minister for Local Government, (first elected for Donegal in 1948), who, unlike the Dubliners Haughey and Colley, had considerable support among rural deputies, the party seemed deadlocked. Eventually there emerged a compromise candidate with longer experience of office than the others, Jack Lynch, Minister for Finance (deputy for Cork City since 1948 and appointed a parliamentary secretary in 1951), who had apparently expressed no previous aspirations to lead the party. Blaney and Haughey both withdrew from the race; Lynch was elected to the leadership of the Fianna Fáil Parliamentary Party, by fifty-one votes to Colley's nineteen, and was formally elected Taoiseach on 10 November 1966. He retained all his rivals in senior posts.[31]

Lynch's first serious test came in the electoral field. In 1967 an All-Party Committee was set up, under the chairmanship of George Colley, to make recommendations for 'tidying up' the Constitution (then thirty years old). Its report, which appeared just before the Christmas recess, made a number of agreed recommendations (including the setting up of an independent commission to undertake the periodic task of constituency revision) but, not surprisingly, found itself unable to agree on the electoral system, and merely relegated to several 'annexes' the arguments for and against change, without making any specific recommendation.[32]

The publication of this report, combined with a speech strongly advocating the first-past-the-post system—'the straight vote', as it was now called—by Kevin Boland (who had succeeded Blaney as Minister for Local Government at the change-over in 1966), was taken as evidence of the imminent appearance of another government bill to alter the electoral system, and a spate of newpaper articles appeared in January 1968 on the merits and demerits of STV.[33] In February the Government Information Bureau announced that the government intended to introduce legislation changing the voting system and also widening the tolerance limits in drawing up constituencies. Both bills would, of course, have to be submitted to the people in a referendum.

On 21 February Lynch moved for leave to introduce the two bills, designated the Third and Fourth Amendment to the Constitution Bills; the Third authorising a tolerance of up to 16 per cent of the national average in drawing up constituencies; and the Fourth (like the same of 1959) abolishing STV and replacing it with the 'straight vote'. Both bills would be taken together This formal first stage was passed and the second reading debate (the second stage) was fixed for 28 February.

In his opening speech on the bill,[34] the Taoiseach set the tone for the debate. He pointed out that while the High Court decision of 1961 had been that a tolerance of 19 per cent of the national average was too high, previous constituency revisions had in fact ranged from 11 per cent to 19 per cent and the government wished the more 'realistic' ratio of 16 per cent to be written into the Constitution particularly in order to have some latitude when dealing with the underpopulated west. On the voting system, Lynch's main emphasis differed from that of de Valera in 1959. He asserted that the first question was whether deputies wanted a multiplicity of parties and a series of coalition governments, or single-party government; the second, which system was likely to produce which result? (To that question he said there was only one possible answer, 'if deputies were honest'.) Given the state of the country at that time, with its need for strong government to underpin the continuing economic expansion, they were faced, he said, with three 'majority bent' parties, each committed to securing an overall majority for its own policies, with the consequent danger of electoral deadlock. Thus the argument from the government benches was not, as in 1959, about the weakness and inadequacy of coalition government, but about the difficulty under the existing system, given the characteristics of the three parties, of forming a government at all. This was to be the government's strongest argument during the debates.

For the opposition, Liam Cosgrave who had maintained silence in 1959, now unequivocally stated the Fine Gael viewpoint: the people had already expressed their support for the existing system and there was no point in asking them again; there were far more urgent matters to attend to than changing the method of voting, or 'rigging' the constituencies in favour of particular areas. Brendan Corish argued in a similar manner.

The second reading debate on both bills, while not quite as long as the debate in 1959, extended over twelve full parliamentary days, between 28 February and 3 April 1968.[35] The strictures passed earlier in this book on the quality of the speeches in that year could be repeated here, since most of the deputies were rehashing arguments advanced nine years previously and little fresh evidence was presented. The fact that the tolerance limits were linked to the method of voting allowed the opposition to claim that Fianna Fail was not only seeking the advantages of the straight vote but also planning a large-scale gerrymander. To this, Fianna Fáil replied that the effect of the judicial decisions of 1961 was that some depopulated western counties would soon be too small even for three-seat constituencies, and that it was desirable not to cross county boundaries when drawing up new constituencies, even single-seat ones. Lynch promised that if the Amendments passed, the task of revision would be entrusted to a commission chaired by a judge.

On the committee stage of the Fourth Amendment Bill, an interesting development occurred when Patrick Norton, a Labour deputy (son of the former leader who had died in 1963) introduced an amendment replacing the straight vote in the single-seat constituencies by STV (6 June). The 'Norton Amendment', identical to James Dillon's proposal in 1959, caused considerable embarrassment to Fianna Fáil, who could not deny that in the one country where it was in use for parliamentary elections (Australia) it had provided stable government, but they refused any compromise.[36]

After the bill had passed through the Senate (where Boland made a six-hour speech!) the debate, which had been more or less continuous in the newspapers since the beginning of the year, continued through the summer recess and right up to the date of the referendum (16 October). The main participants were, as in 1959, academics, trade unionists and, of course, politicians who were never satisfied to give the other side the last word. As in 1959, expressed opinion leaned heavily in favour of the status quo. Fears of permanent Fianna Fáil domination reinforced by gerrymandering were continually and skilfully exploited. Apart from the *Irish* (and *Sunday*) *Press,* the main newspapers were strongly against change. The *Irish Times* maintained its pro-PR stance with a confidence not evident in the earlier campaign. The *Independent,* under a new editor, was not afraid to commit itself on the same side.[37] The profusion of academic participants in the debate was notable, and, as far as can be ascertained, only Professor Ferdinand Hermens and the present writer indicated that an academic argument *could* be made for the 'straight vote'.[38] Miss Lakeman again campaigned with undiminished energy for the retention of STV.

In one respect the campaign in the country was markedly different from that of 1959. This was through the involvement of Radio Telefís Eireann. As mentioned earlier, the structure of the Irish television service made it subject to direction by the Minister for Posts and Telegraphs—and thus less independent than the BBC.[39] In its early years Ministers interpreted their duties paternalistically, occasionally even trying to alter the content of news items; and during the debates on the Third and Fourth Amendments an allegation was made by a Labour deputy—and not contradicted—that an internal memorandum was circulating within the service prohibiting any discussion of the pros and cons of the electoral question.[40] (It might be remembered that it was as late as 1956 that the BBC felt free to comment on British electoral politics!) However, this injunction, if it existed, was breached, at least in spirit, when the current affairs department of RTE boldly arranged several discussions on the issue shortly before the referendum.

On 16 October 1968, voting took place on both the Third and Fourth Amendments. The turnout was higher than in 1959—65.8 per cent compared to 58.3 per cent—and the voting on both Amendments was virtually identical: of 1.081 million votes cast, 424,000 (39.2 per cent) were for the Third Amendment and 657,000 (60.8 per cent) against; 423,000 (39.2 per cent) for the Fourth Amendment and 658,000 (60.8 per cent) against. Thus the two Amendments were defeated by a majority of over 20 per cent. Only four constituencies registered majorities in favour of the Amendments—Clare, West Galway and the two Donegal constituencies—while thirty-four returned adverse majorities, the 'no' vote being especially high in Dublin and Cork.[41]

69

The Lynch government had no choice but to accept defeat, and since 1968 scarcely a voice has been raised to suggest a further reform of the method of voting in the Republic.

(b) Following the defeat of the Constitutional Amendments the government, as they had promised during the campaign, introduced another constituency revision bill to take account of the recent population movements. A week after the referendum (23 October) Kevin Boland moved for leave to introduce the Electoral (Amendment) Bill, 1968.

The bill was published on 12 November and the second reading debate opened on 27 November.[42] When they saw the text of the bill, both opposition parties raised a concerted howl of protest. The bill made no change in the total number of deputies (144), but increased the number of constituencies from thirty-eight to forty-two. Instead of nine 5-seat, twelve 4-seat and seventeen 3-seat constituencies, the bill kept only two 5-seaters (Carlow-Kilkenny and Laois-Offaly); increased the number of 4-seaters to fourteen, and the 3-seaters to twenty-six. But it was the location of these constituencies that aroused most comment. Dublin City and County, where Fianna Fáil rarely exceeded 40 per cent of the vote in the previous constituencies, was split into eight 4-seaters and two 3-seaters; while in the west, south, and three Ulster counties (where its average performance approached 50 per cent) the bill established four 4-seaters and twenty 3-seaters. The opposition were not slow to draw the appropriate inference—that Fianna Fáil were introducing three-seaters where they were strong and four-seaters where they were weak.

To forestall the second stage of the bill, T. J. Fitzpatrick (Fine Gael spokesman on local government) introduced a private members' bill on 20 November, entrusting the task of revision to a constituency commission comprising three deputies from each side of the House, and under the chairmanship of a Supreme or High Court judge.[43] This was substantially the same type of commission as Lynch had proposed in connection with the Third Amendment. The Labour Party supported Fitzpatrick's bill as 'the proper way' to draw up constituencies; but Boland gave two reasons for opposing it:

1. He was 'advised' that Article 16.2.1. ('Dail Eireann shall be composed of members who represent constituencies determined by law') precluded the handing-over of this function to a commission. (If so, why was a consequential amendment to Article 16.2.1. not incorporated with the Third and Fourth Amendments?)

2. Fine Gael inconsistency. Boland quoted from a speech by T. F. O'Higgins during the 1959 referendum debates rejecting a commission; but Fitzpatrick angrily rejoined that in the recent debates *he* had supported the idea. Leave to introduce was refused by sixty-five votes to forty-nine. Thus when the second stage began, the Minister met a more consistently hostile response from the opposition parties than had greeted any previous

constituency revision. There had always been objections from deputies to losing parts of 'their' territory, and the smaller parties had also objected to the progressive elimination of the very large constituencies, but to quote Michael Gallagher, 'Despite allegations that Fianna Fáil had done this [gerrymandering] at several revisions, only the 1969 revision seems to have been designed in this spirit'.[44] It was also, of course, the first revision to be made before it was constitutionally due.

There were vehement objections to the way in which counties were 'butchered'. The 'Boland Gerrymander' (as the opposition constantly called it) involved taking seventeen pieces of territory from nine counties and affected 100,000 people—for example, it suggested partitioning Leitrim between Sligo, Donegal and Roscommon; merging North Clare and South Galway and putting part of Roscommon into the new constituency of North-East Galway. (One Labour deputy, James Tully—later to become famous for another constituency revision—said: 'I have a personal view on this. I believe that county boundaries are important just as I believe the national boundary is important . . . I do not agree that county boundaries should be sundered'.[45] But another Labour deputy said that people were not concerned about county boundaries, except perhaps in the matter of hurling and football, or lowering the rates.)

All these points were made forcefully during the three full days of the second reading debate. Alternative schemes were also proposed, one from the floor of the House by a Fine Gael deputy; another much-cited one had been presented in the *Sunday Independent* (19 November) by Senator Garret FitzGerald, which while keeping within the tolerance limits—1,000 people on either side of the national average of 20,100 per deputy—would only affect 40,000 people. Some Fianna Fáil deputies also expressed lack of enthusiasm for the bill, especially those from the west which was losing three seats, and one deputy complained that his constituency was now over a hundred miles long!

Both in his opening and closing speeches in the debate Boland made much the same points.[46] He emphasised that under the High Court ruling, twenty-four of the existing constituencies were outside the tolerance limits; there was no alternative to breaching county boundaries—both Leitrim (pop. 30,000) and Sligo (pop. 51,000) were too small even for three-seaters, while Clare was too small for a four-seater and too large for a three-seater; the alternative schemes would also have cut across county boundaries and would, in fact, also have taken three seats from the west and given four seats to the Dublin conurbation; and furthermore five-seat constituencies were 'unwieldy in practice'. But he made no attempt to explain the distribution of the three- and four-seat constituencies. The second stage passed narrowly by sixty votes to fifty-eight, just before the Christmas recess, on 11 December 1968.

The committee stage was brief (5, 11 and 12 February 1969) and the bill passed through the rest of the Dáil stages and the Senate unchanged, except for some drafting amendments proposed by the Minister. The Electoral (Amendment) Act became law on 26 March 1969.

(c) On 21 May 1969, as expected, Lynch announced a dissolution with polling on 18 June. The three parties—for no minor party candidates appeared and there were only twenty-seven Independents—entered the campaign in very different moods. The Labour Party had at last come out in true socialist colours;[47] Brendan Corish's policy statement of 1967, boldly advocating extensive state control and 'workers' democracy', and denouncing the 'greed and exploitation' of the capitalist system, became the party's electoral programme. It has been argued that the appearance of such a left-wing programme from a major party would have been unthinkable in Ireland before the pontificate of Pope John XXIII. Be that as it may, the party had made great strides since 1965; membership had gone up from 9,000 in 1966 to 15,300 in 1969; ancient quarrels had been made up by the re-affiliation to the party of the ITGWU (still the biggest union in the Republic) and the affiliation of its old rival, the Workers Union of Ireland, and, most significant of all, in the 1967 local elections Labour had done well in all the major urban areas, displacing Fine Gael as the main opposition party in both Dublin and Cork.

Emboldened by these successes, Corish prepared for the great break-through. Labour put up ninety-nine candidates (as against forty-two in 1965) and for the first time contested every constituency (eight constituencies had had no Labour candidate in 1965 and eleven in 1961). The candidates included such well-known intellectuals as Dr Conor Cruise O'Brien (just back from New York), Dr David Thornley and Mr Justin Keating (both television personalities), Dr Noel Browne and Dr John O'Donovan. The Labour campaign was marked by a new professionalism. Unlike the drab manifestos of the past, the election programme appeared as a well-produced booklet with a glossy cover, and a special broadsheet entitled *Election News* was also published during the campaign. Party spokesmen claimed (like Clann na Poblachta in 1948) that they were putting up enough candidates to form a single-party government. Corish wrote: 'This time Labour goes for government,' adding, 'Ireland will have a Labour government . . . soon. Because it must have.' The party paper also announced that after the election Corish would be nominated as Taoiseach, and if he did not get a majority then the two 'civil war parties' would have the responsibility of forming a government between them.[48]

Fine Gael entered the election in a very different frame of mind. Although the party was pleased by the defeat of the government in the referendum, and also by the remarkable performance in the 1966 presidential election of its candidate, T. F. O'Higgins, who came within 10,000 votes of defeating de Valera (then seeking a second seven-year term at the age of eighty-four), it was clear that the momentum gained by the commitment to *The Just Society* had been spent. The leader, Liam Cosgrave, was an unspectacular figure with strong conservative instincts and little sympathy with the ideas of Declan Costello (who, incidentally, did not stand again in 1969).[49] Fine Gael spokesmen were profoundly irritated by their erstwhile Labour colleagues regarding them as no different from Fianna Fáil. It must here be pointed out that Labour did not have a monopoly of academic talent. Dr Garret FitzGerald and Professor John Kelly (both standing for the first time as Dáil candidates) were as trenchant and forceful speakers as any of the Labour team. But during the campaign Fine Gael appeared to be fighting on two fronts.[50] On the one hand, they excoriated Fianna Fáil for inadequacies in their social policy—especially concerning public-funded housing which had drastically declined since 1957. But they also took a series of side-swipes at Labour for their 'absurd pretensions' (Cosgrave). FitzGerald pointed out that Fine Gael *was* the only alternative government to Fianna Fáil, and Kelly claimed that while his party wanted office *then,* Labour appeared to be satisfied with the role of 'progressive opposition' until the 1980s! Relations between the two opposition parties were at the lowest ebb since 1948. The Fine Gael programme was not very inspiring. Apart from minor reforms (such as an ombudsman) and the reiteration of the 1961 pledge to abolish compulsory Irish, there was little to enthuse the voters.

Fianna Fáil had apparently completely recovered from their referendum set back. Their campaign, directed by Charles Haughey, concentrated on Labour as the real enemy and wrote off Fine Gael as 'dead'—to the great indignation of the latter. In Fianna Fáil speeches, Labour's proposals were given a marxist colouring; they were seeking to nationalise land; they were allegedly admirers of Castro's Cuba. Fianna Fáil also made great play with the commitment by their late Minister for Education, Donogh O'Malley, to universal secondary education; and they generally represented themselves as the only party really capable of providing a government. Lynch also made a successful speaking tour.

Two newspapers followed predictable lines, the *Irish Press* uncritically for Fianna Fáil, the *Independent* against; while the *Irish Times* found the election 'perplexing' in that the differences between Fianna Fáil and Fine Gael were becoming increasingly difficult to determine, and Labour was so resolutely against coalition (18 June).

When the ballots were counted it was seen that Fianna Fáil had broken all records by winning four successive regular general elections and had also increased its majority. Fianna Fáil actually dropped 2 per cent in its share of the poll but gained two seats; Fine Gael, with the same percentage as in 1965 (34.1 per cent), gained three seats; but Labour, in spite of all its efforts and an increased share of the vote (15.4 per cent to 17.0 per cent), fell from twenty-one to eighteen seats. The Labour vote rose considerably in Dublin, where in six out of ten constituencies it ran ahead of Fine Gael and all the Dublin intellectuals were returned; but this was poor compensation for losses in rural areas where its radical policies did not seem to attract much support.[51]

The extreme disproportionality of the result will be examined later. Suffice it to say here that apart from the constituency revision (to which some commentators gave the chief credit for the Fianna Fáil victory), the leakage of Labour votes to Fianna Fáil, and the proportion of non-transferables were also significant factors. A work published in 1973 estimated that seven seats were 'vulnerable to a cooperative effort in vote transference between Fine Gael and Labour'.[52] That this cooperation did not occur was not surprising in view of the cool relations between the parties during the election.

After the results the *Irish Times* perceptively assessed the Corish gamble as a failure, and predicted that he would shortly be faced with the most serious decision of his life—the future direction of a 'majority bent' party, aiming to govern, but apparently doomed to perpetual minority party status.[53] Finally, it is worth mentioning that the 1969 election marked the end of the political careers of two former Taoisigh and a former party leader, none of whom offered themselves for re-election. They were John A. Costello who had been an active back-bencher for ten years (he spoke on the electoral question in 1968 with undiminished vigour); James Dillon (who had also served on the backbenches since 1965) and Sean Lemass, then a sick man, who had played virtually no part in Dáil proceedings since his resignation in 1966.

III

1969-73

This period in Irish politics is so recent that only those events with direct electoral significance will be discussed in this section.

(a) The Lynch government with its clear Dáil majority took advantage of the resignation of de Gaulle in June 1969 and the more conciliatory attitude of his successor M. Georges Pompidou, to make yet another application to join the EEC, together with the United Kingdom, Denmark and Norway. This time all was plain sailing. When the original applications of 1961 had been reactivated in 1967, the EEC Commission had issued a statement to the effect that all four applicants were sufficiently advanced for full membership. Negotiations were re-opened late in 1969, and continued *pari passu* with the other countries until 1972, when Ireland signed the Treaty of Rome. As in the case of Norway and Denmark, Irish accession to the Community required a referendum, to amend the Article of the Constitution (15.2.1) which vested legislative power solely in the Oireachtas (parliament). The bill—yet another Third Amendment to the Constitution Bill—passed quickly through both Houses, and the referendum was fixed for 10 May. Fine Gael supported the government, and opposition came only from Labour and a revitalised Sinn Féin (of which more later), on similar grounds as the left wing of the British Labour Party invoked against entry: that the Community was a 'rich man's club'; that protected Irish industry would be unable to withstand the stiff wind of European competition; that the Treaty involved a surrender of sovereignty and economic self-determination. However, government propaganda was much more forceful: the central point was that if Britain joined, Ireland simply could not afford to stay out and the advantages to the country of an expanding export market were also emphasised. The Labour Party campaign was half-hearted, and Sinn Féin appeared as backward-looking nationalists. On polling day there was a turnout of 70.9 per cent—higher than at any previous referendum; 83.1 per cent voted in favour of entry and the adverse vote was almost identical to the Labour share of the poll in 1969. The party immediately declared its acceptance of the popular verdict and the question was closed.

(b) The alarming developments in Northern Ireland in 1969 helped to precipitate a crisis which rocked the Fianna Fáil government and party. The eruptive factor was the rioting in Derry and Belfast in the week 10-17 August 1969, which resulted in the first casualties of the current 'Troubles'. Lynch's first reaction, his 'we won't stand idly by' speech and his request for UN support undoubtedly gave the impression in Northern Ireland that active intervention by the Irish army was probable, if not imminent. It is true that after British troops had been sent into the Catholic areas of Belfast and Derry, Lynch made a much more moderate speech, in Tralee, but it did not remove the impression left by his previous utterances.[54]

Although for the rest of 1969 and early 1970 there was little violence in Northern Ireland and political optimists hoped that local government reform (feverishly rushed through Stormont by the Chichester-Clark government) would restore peace, two ominous developments in the Republic suggested otherwise.

In December 1969 a convention of Sinn Féin (which had been moribund since the early 1960s but revived during the Northern crisis) in Dublin resulted in a schism in the movement. The majority, claiming the title of 'Official Sinn Féin', declared their willingness to participate in constitutional politics in the South, while not renouncing violence as a means of ending Partition. A minority regarded this as a betrayal of the old tradition of abstention from both 'partitionist' legislatures, seceded from the movement, and set up their own organisation which they called 'Provisional Sinn Féin'. Both organisations had military wings operating in Northern Ireland, the Official and Provisional IRA, of which the latter proved the more extreme.[55]

It was common knowledge, during the lull in early 1970, that arms for the Provisionals were coming into Ireland from American sympathisers. But the country was staggered by the sequence of events in the first two weeks of May. First, on 5 May, the Minister for Justice resigned for health reasons. Then, on 7 May, the Taoiseach announced that he had dismissed two of his most powerful Ministers, Charles Haughey, Minister for Finance, and Neil Blaney, Minister for Agriculture, for alleged involvement in the illegal importation of arms. A thunderstruck Dáil was informed by Lynch that the two ex-Ministers would stand trial for this alleged criminal offence. On the same day, Kevin Boland resigned as Minister for Local Government, out of sympathy for Blaney and Haughey, and on 8 May he was followed by his parliamentary secretary.

Thus, within one week, the Cabinet lost four Ministers, more than at any time since the Army mutiny of 1924,[56] and Fianna Fáil faced the first internal crisis in its history. The 'Arms Trial', after the manner of Irish political trials, resulted in the acquittal of all the defendants; but the rift within Fianna Fáil was deepened since one of their former ministerial colleagues gave evidence that flatly contradicted the defendants on a number of points.

After the Arms Trial the careers of the ex-Ministers diverged. Boland and Blaney at first tried to dislodge Lynch from the leadership of Fianna Fáil and persuade the party to adopt a 'tough' policy towards Northern Ireland. When the government forced a vote of confidence in the Dáil in November 1970, Blaney supported it while Boland, rather than support it, resigned his seat—a futile gesture, since he did not offer himself for re-election, and the by-election was won by Fine Gael. At the Ard Fheis in 1971, the Boland faction was decisively beaten in an attempt to pass a vote of no confidence in the leadership; that was the stormiest Ard Fheis in the party's history, and although Lynch got a hearing some of his colleagues did not. Then Boland left Fianna Fáil to found a 'traditionally republican' party, called Aontacht Eireann (Irish Unity). Just one (Fianna Fáil) deputy joined it, but it then began to prepare for the next general election.

Meanwhile, Blaney and the ex-parliamentary secretary, Paudge Brennan, continued to snipe at official Fianna Fáil policy on Northern Ireland both inside and outside the Dáil. They were both, in consequence, successively expelled from the Parliamentary Party and the National Party (June and December 1972). Haughey, on the other hand, refrained from criticism of the official policy, and his rehabilitation within the party began with his election as vice-president at the 1972 Ard Fheis.

After the 1971 Ard Fheis it was clear that the existing leadership had survived, but at a high price in internal party dissension. Through defections—altogether five deputies had either left or been expelled from the party[57]—the Lynch government was now in a minority. The Northern problem continued to worry the government for the rest of its term of office, particularly after March 1972 when the Stormont regime was suspended by the Heath government and Provisional IRA violence reached its peak. The government was embarrassed by the facility with which raiders from the North found refuge in the Republic, and the freedom with which Provisional Sinn Féin headquarters in Dublin publicised the activities of their colleagues in the North. Eventually, in November 1972, the government introduced an Offences against the State (Amendment) Bill, making it easier to take proceedings against illegal organisations, including the Provisional IRA. While Labour opposed the bill as an unnecessary encroachment on the rights of the citizen, Fine Gael were divided—and their support would be necessary to carry the bill, since all the ex-Fianna Fáil deputies could be expected to vote against. On the day of the second reading division (1 December) there occurred the first bombing of Dublin which brought home to the people the grim realities of the Northern situation. Cosgrave thereupon swung the Fine Gael party firmly behind the bill and it passed into law.

(c) Early in the life of the Nineteenth Dáil there were signs that Labour had learnt a rueful lesson from the 1969 election results and were moving towards a new accommodation with Fine Gael. The formal decision was taken against strong opposition, at the annual Conference in December 1970 in Cork, where the Party had adopted the 'go-it-alone' policy thirteen years before. But it appears that the crucial decision was taken some days earlier at a stormy private meeting of the Parliamentary Party, at which Corish persuaded his reluctant colleagues that a new coalition would be in the best interests of the country.[58] Soon afterwards informal contacts were established. The negotiations got off to a slow start because Labour's negative attitude towards the EEC posed an obstacle, but after May 1972, contacts became more frequent.

(d) On 7 December 1972 (just after the passing of the Offences against the State Bill), two further referenda were held on constitutional amendments; the first on a bill to lower the minimum voting age to eighteen, in line with other western democracies; the second to delete the part of Article 44, referring to the 'special position' of the Roman Catholic church, to which Protestants had frequently objected. In a low poll (50.6 per cent) the two were carried by 84.6 per cent and 84.4 per cent respectively, and became the Fourth and Fifth Amendments to the Constitution.

The new register, on which an estimated 120,000 new voters would be enrolled would not come into operation until April 1973. However, on 5 February, during the Christmas recess, Lynch announced a dissolution, with polling on 28 February, and the turbulent life of the Nineteenth Dáil came to an end.

IV
THE GENERAL ELECTION OF 1973

The suddenness of the dissolution, coupled with the fact that only three weeks were allowed for campaigning, acted as a spur to Fine Gael and Labour. On 7 February the negotiations were concluded with the publication of a 'Statement of Intent', in effect a joint electoral manifesto, committing the parties to the goal of 'a modern progressive society based on social justice'. Its fourteen points were reminiscent of *The Just Society*, including higher welfare benefits, reduction of the pensionable age, pro-

77

gressive abolition of rates, abolition of death duties, stabilisation of prices and also 'protection of the liberty and safety of the individual and the democratic institutions of the State' and 'the promotion of a peaceful solution in the North'.

The prospect of another coalition with Fine Gael[59] was too much for a section of the Labour Party (calling itself the Liaison Committee of the Left), which claimed that the Labour movement had not given a mandate for a pre-election pact. Browne announced that he would not stand as a Coalition candidate,[60] but Thornley, with some misgivings, accepted the 'Statement of Intent'.

The Coalition manifesto in effect became the basis for the campaign. Fianna Fáil's attempt to make Northern Ireland an issue on the ground that only they could handle that delicate situation was stymied by the Coalition parties' concentration on economic and social problems. However, the Northern policy was attacked from many quarters—by Aontacht Eireann, who put up thirteen candidates, including Kevin Boland, mainly in Dublin (apart from advocating a strong Republican policy on the North Aontacht Eireann seemed to have very few ideas of its own); by Official Sinn Féin which nominated ten candidates and whose policy, apart from Irish reunification, was strongly socialist; and also by Blaney and the five other Independent (ex-Fianna Fáil) candidates.

The Coalition also replied to Fianna Fáil claims for the success of its Northern policy by stressing that neither Fine Gael nor Labour suffered from internal strife, and that even after the expulsions Fianna Fáil harboured more militant Republicans within its ranks than it would like to admit. The conduct of various senior Ministers also came under veiled attack from many Coalition spokesmen. But there was no ambiguity about Conor Cruise O'Brien's charges of Fianna Fáil vacillation, the ever-present danger of a takeover by the Blaneyites, and the equivocal position of Charles Haughey, an acknowledged candidate for the leadership. Apart from O'Brien and Keating, the Labour intellectuals did not figure prominently in the campaign.

Fianna Fáil's manifesto, as might be expected from a party that had been in office for sixteen years, was unimaginative and relied too much on past achievements. So their candidates spent much time on questioning the credibility of the Coalition's social programme. The Coalition claimed that the programme could be funded by expected grants of some £30 million from the EEC Regional Fund, without any extra taxation. Fianna Fáil dismissed this claim and alleged that an annual increase in general taxation of the order of £70 million would be required. However, a turning point in the campaign came on 21 February, when Lynch announced, in defiance of all previous Fianna Fáil pronouncements on the subject, that rates *could* be abolished, that Fianna Fáil would abolish them in the following year, and that they would also channel into welfare all the funds available from EEC entry. A few days later, in one of the regular television confrontations, Garret FitzGerald was able to produce before an almost speechless George Colley (Minister for Finance and Fianna Fáil director of elections) an advertisement from the *Limerick Leader*[61] on behalf of the local Fianna Fáil candidates (including a Minister), which had appeared *after* Mr Lynch's statement, attacking as nonsensical the Coalition pledge to abolish rates! The volte-face on rates dominated the last days of the campaign.

Some interesting points of election law were raised during the campaign. One arose from the provisions of the Electoral Act, 1963, which for the first time authorised candidates to mention their party affiliations on the ballot paper—provided they appeared on a Register of Political Parties to be kept and annually revised by the Clerk of the Dáil, who before registering had to be satisfied that the party was (a) a 'genuine' political party and (b) organised to contest a Dáil or a local election. Sean D. Loftus, a Dublin barrister, who had already lost four deposits in seeking election as a 'Christian Democrat', was so angered by the refusal of the Clerk of the Dáil to register his party that he changed his name by deed poll to include the appellations 'Christian Democrat' and also 'Dublin Bay' (which he was interested in protecting from oil developers) so that on the ballot papers in the Dublin North Central constituency he appeared as 'Christian Democrat Dublin Bay Loftus, Sean D. (He lost another deposit but this was not the end of Mr Loftus's political aspirations.)[62]

Also at the beginning of the campaign, a twenty-year-old student sought a High Court injunction against the Attorney General, claiming that he was entitled to vote under the Fourth Amendment. The court decided against him, though expressing some sympathy for his claim. (Lynch's explanation, incidentally, for holding the election on the old register was that it had to be out of the way before the presidential election, constitutionally due in June.)

The total number of candidates was 334 (372 in 1969). Declan Costello stood again for Fine Gael, in Dublin South-West. But two familiar figures were missing, the ex-Tanaiste, Frank Aiken, who retired after fifty years as a deputy for Louth, and Thomas F. O'Higgins, deputy leader of Fine Gael, who announced that he would not defend his Dublin seat but would concentrate instead on the forthcoming presidential election for which he had again been chosen as his party's candidate.

As in the previous elections, there was sustained media coverage of the campaign from all angles. At the beginning Fianna Fáil appeared to be doing well, but towards the end, especially after the *Limerick Leader* gaffe, the Coalition seemed more confident and paid little regard to the time-worn Fianna Fáil warnings about the weakness and ineptitude of coalitions. To a much greater extent than ever before, Fine Gael and Labour candidates worked as a team, and in newspaper advertisements both parties strongly advised their supporters to vote solidly for Coalition candidates.

The newspapers adopted a more sophisticated approach than in earlier elections. The *Irish Press,* as always was enthusiastically pro-Fianna Fáil. The *Independent,* with a new political commentator, gave ample space to an opinion poll taken a few days before polling, which showed an overwhelming majority of voters concerned about bread-and-butter issues (especially prices), to the exclusion of Northern Ireland and the security problem—the commentator's piece was headed 'Prices may sink Lynch' (26 February). The *Irish Times* was enthusiastically pro-Coalition, both on theoretical grounds—coalitions were *not* inherently unstable and were far preferable to a continual monopoly of power by one party—and also on account of the quality of the Coalition policies (20 February). A change of government in 1973, the *Times* averred, would be just as compatible with stability as in 1932 (26 February). At the end of the campaign the *Irish Times* magisterially pronounced that the Coalition might not win the election, but that it had won the argument (27 February).

The result was a triumph for the Coalitionists. In a turnout of 76.6 per cent, Fianna Fáil actually improved slightly on its 1969 share of the vote, but lost six seats! Fine Gael, with an increase of merely 1 per cent in votes, went up from fifty to fifty-four seats, the highest number since its foundation; while Labour gained a seat, although dropping from 17 per cent to 13.7 per cent of the poll. Minor parties and dissidents fared badly. Although Blaney headed the poll in his Donegal constituency, all the others expelled from Fianna Fáil were defeated. Aontacht Eireann's one outgoing deputy lost his seat and the remaining candidates, including Boland, lost their deposits. A similar fate befell Sinn Féin—with nine lost deposits out of ten candidates. The greatest surprise of the campaign was the defeat of Brian Lenihan, Minister for Foreign Affairs.[63] Declan Costello got back easily, but John O'Donovan lost his seat.

The high level of solidarity among the Fine Gael and Labour voters neutralised the traditional advantage Fianna Fáil had enjoyed in the rural areas, especially the three-seaters. In three 3-seat constituencies (Kildare, West Mayo and Sligo-Leitrim) Fianna Fáil, with over 50 per cent of the first preferences, failed to win more than one seat. There were also marginal losses by Fianna Fáil in Laois-Offaly, Longford-Westmeath, Roscommon-Leitrim (Lenihan's seat), North Tipperary and Waterford. Five of these gains were by Fine Gael and three by Labour. Fine Gael also won seats from Labour in three Dublin constituencies and easily re-established itself as the second largest party in the Dublin area, being ahead of Labour in eight out of ten constituencies.[64]

The drop in the Labour share of the vote (the lowest since 1961) and the loss of seats to Fine Gael, barely compensated for by the winning of seats from Fianna Fáil (through heavy transfers from Fine Gael candidates), came as a great disappointment to the party—and was instantly seized upon by Labour dissidents as proof of the unpopularity of the Coalition arrangement among their customary supporters. Nevertheless, with a majority of five seats over Fianna Fáil, the National Coalition took over on the first day of the Twentieth Dáil. Cosgrave became Taoiseach and Corish Tanaiste; and the strong position of Fine Gael in relation to its partner was evident in the allocation of portfolios—Fine Gael taking ten ministries, including Finance, Foreign Affairs, Agriculture and Education, to Labour's five. One of the first policies implemented by the Coalition was the old Fine Gael pledge to abolish Irish as a compulsory subject for a Leaving Certificate award, and as a test for entry to the public service.

V
1973-7

(a) In June 1973, at the end of his second term in the Presidency, Eamon de Valera finally retired from public life, at the age of ninety-one. The result of the presidential election disappointed the Coalition. In spite of full support by both parties, the Fine Gael candidate, Thomas F. O'Higgins, who had done so well in 1966, was easily beaten by Erskine Childers, the former Tanaiste, who received 636,161 votes (52 per cent) to O'Higgins' 587,577 (48 per cent). But as previous results had showed, presidential elections are no more accurate a barometer of party strength than are local ones.[65] (Childers died in office in December 1974, while O'Higgins, after a brief period as a High Court judge, was appointed Chief Justice in 1974.)

(b) The first year of the Coalition was dominated by the Ulster problem, as 1972 had been. The Sunningdale Agreement (December 1973), in which the government of the Republic was for the first time involved in constitutional arrangements for Northern Ireland, raised false hopes which were rudely dashed by the collapse of the 'power-sharing' Executive in May 1974, following the general strike called by the extreme loyalists. After the collapse of the Executive and the reversion to direct rule, the Coalition adopted towards Northern Ireland a public policy of inaction; but behind the scenes, through the quiet and persistent diplomacy of the Foreign Minister, Garret FitzGerald, they managed to place Anglo-Irish relations on a better footing than for many years. On the other hand the government adopted a stern attitude towards the IRA, intensifying repressive legislation through a series of measures culminating in two bills in September 1976, which increased sentences for recruiting for illegal organisations and extended the period of detention without trial to seven days. These measures were stoutly defended by the Taoiseach, the Minister for Justice (Patrick Cooney) and Dr Conor Cruise O'Brien who, though not directly concerned with law and order (his portfolio was Posts and Telegraphs), spoke frequently of the danger posed by illegal armies to any modern democratic state, and banned from RTE any publicity for Provisional Sinn Féin/IRA activities. The government claimed—especially after the firm reaction to the kidnapping of the Dutch industrialist, Dr Tiede Herrema in

October 1975—that they were adopting a much firmer attitude towards subversives than Fianna Fáil had done, but some Labour deputies, especially Dr John O'Connell and Dr David Thornley, were unhappy about the party's change of policy on civil rights. Some indiscreet utterances by Ministers in 1976 about the necessity for 'responsible' reporting were widely interpreted by the anti-government papers, the *Irish Press* and *Hibernia*, as the prelude to press censorship.[66]

(c) After entry to the EEC in January 1973, the Republic was fully involved in the Community institutions through its representatives on the Council of Ministers (especially FitzGerald), the Commission (the ex-Fianna Fáil Minister, Dr P. J. Hillery), the Court (the ex-Chief Justice, Cearbhall O Dalaigh), and some ten deputies and senators in the Assembly, where Fine Gael sat with the Christian Democrat Group, Labour with the Socialists and Fianna Fáil with the Gaullists. The holding of a Community summit in Dublin in March 1975 marked the virtual ending of the isolationist tradition.

(d) Like every other western state, Ireland was hit by the quadrupling of oil prices at the end of 1973. This led to severe domestic inflation between mid-1974 and mid-1975, with average wage increases of 30 per cent. The government reacted with a supplementary budget in 1975 which tried to help the lower income groups by food subsidies, and to hold wage demands to a reasonable figure. Social benefits were also increased; but in return were two imposts likely to antagonise traditional Fine Gael supporters: direct taxation of farmers and a capital gains tax. All these measures to combat domestic inflation could not affect import prices, which continued to rise, particularly in 1976, with consequential effects on domestic prices.

Another apparently insoluble problem was posed by the continuing population explosion and the virtual closing of the emigration safety valve. At the end of 1976 there were 111,000 registered unemployed (almost twice as many as in 1973),[67] while over half the population was under the age of twenty-six.

(e) When President Childers died suddenly at the end of 1974 the government was not at all anxious for a contested election, and did not nominate a candidate. Within Fianna Fáil, after an abortive attempt to draft Jack Lynch (whose leadership had been somewhat lethargic since the general election), the party invited the EEC Judge, Cearbhall O Dalaigh, to stand. (He had been an unsuccessful Fianna Fáil candidate for the Dáil in the 1940s and served as Attorney General between 1951 and 1953). O Dalaigh was returned unopposed. However his presidency also ended prematurely, owing to a bizarre incident in 1976. The President had exercised his right under the Constitution to refer to the Supreme Court the Emergency Powers Bill which increased the powers of the police, most notably by extending the period of detention from forty-eight hours to seven days—and when the Court confirmed that the bill was constitutional, it was signed by the President and became law (16 October 1976).

82

That should have closed the question, but on 18 October, in a speech at an army barracks, the Minister for Defence, Patrick Donegan, referred to the President as a 'thundering disgrace'. On being questioned in the Dáil about the insult to the President, the Taoiseach indicated that the Minister had offered to apologise to the President, but he did not issue any public rebuke, nor did he apologise on behalf of the government. On 22 October, the President resigned and released to the press a stinging reply which he had sent to a qualified apology from the Minister. Only after Ó Dalaigh's resignation did Cosgrave reveal that Donegan too had offered to resign (28 October).

The resignation of President Ó Dalaigh was followed by a storm of protest in the newspapers, most correspondents denouncing both Cosgrave and Donegan for a violation of common constitutional practice in parliamentary democracies.[68] In the ensuing election the Coalition again refrained from putting up a candidate and Dr P. J. Hillery, then EEC Commissioner, became the fifth Fianna Fáil nominee to reach the Presidency, in November 1976.

(f) The extension to Ireland of professional surveys of political opinion was a development of great interest to students of politics. In April 1969, just before the general election, Gallup conducted the first ever survey of party support, broken down into the established categories of class, age and sex. (*See chapter 8.*) Of greater long-term importance was the institution, in November 1974, by Irish Marketing Surveys of monthly polls of first preference voting intentions. From then until the dissolution of the Twentieth Dáil, these polls showed Fianna Fáil ahead of the Coalition, except for two brief periods, and, occasionally in 1976, by as much as 10 percentage points.[69]

Strange to say, these findings attracted no more attention than had the famous Gallup prediction of a Labour victory in Britain some thirty years before.

VI

THE GENERAL ELECTION OF 1977

'I cannot improve on it anyway. I think it is great. Fantastic.'
Mr James Tully, on the Electoral (Amendment)
(No. 2) Bill, 1973 (*Dáil Debates* vol. 268, 2048.)

(a) The run-up to the general election of 1977 may be regarded from one point of view as having started on the second sitting day of the Dáil elected in 1973, when the new Minister for Local Government, James Tully (Labour), moved for leave to introduce a bill to revise the constituencies and stated that the second stage would be taken immediately after the Easter recess.[70] Leave was granted without a division; the census of

1971 had revealed an increase of over 3 per cent in the population and it was known that the previous government had intended to introduce their own bill.

The Electoral (Amendment) (No. 2) Bill, 1973 did not in fact come up for a second reading until 15 November, long after the promised date. Its provisions may be summarised as follows:

The total number of Dáil seats was increased from 144 to 148; but the number of constituencies remained at forty-two—twenty-six 3-seat (as in 1969), ten 4-seat and six 5-seat divisions. Dublin City and County (where the average share of the vote secured by the Coalition parties in 1973 had been 53.6 per cent) was divided into thirteen 3-seaters and one 4-seater (Dun Laoghaire, where in 1973 they had won three out of four seats). In Connacht and the three Ulster counties, where Fianna Fáil support was traditionally strong, there were only four 3-seaters, two 4-seaters and two 5-seaters. County Galway, previously divided into two 3-seaters (in both of which the Coalition had won only one seat in 1973) was re-divided into two 4-seat constituencies, Galway West being topped up with about 9,000 voters from Clare. Outside the Dublin conurbation, with very few exceptions, three-seat constituencies were retained only where the Coalition parties had won, or came close to winning, two seats in the previous election. In the judicious words of one scholar, 'The Coalition's 1974 Electoral Act appears to mark an attempt to maximise its own parliamentary strength at the next election'.[71]

The reaction of Fianna Fáil was anything but judicious. Opening the second reading debate, Tully had made a brief speech, pointing out that frequent population movements necessitated constituency revisions after every census and not just every twelve years, and that there was no dispute between the parties on this point; adverting to the difficulty of attaining population equality, and expressing the quite unrealistic hope that the bill would receive general acceptance in the Dáil and the country.[72] Robert Molloy, the ex-Minister for Local Government, then denounced the bill as 'the most shameful piece of gerrymandering that has been carried out in any part of the country at any time'.[73] He reminded Fine Gael and Labour (including Tully) of the speeches they had made in favour of a boundary commission in 1969; he pointed out that while Tully had said (also in 1969) that he was in favour of keeping county boundaries, wherever possible, in their scheme in eight constituencies bits of one county were added to another; he pointed out that west of the Shannon the ratio of deputies to population was higher than in the Dublin area—which had got the extra four seats; he read extracts from an article by Garret FitzGerald (November 1972) deploring constituency manipulation and expressing admiration for the Boundary Commission in Northern Ireland. To this lengthy speech the only front-bench reply came from Professor John Kelly (a parliamentary secretary), who accepted Molloy's claim that the people *could* show their revulsion against the scheme by giving Fianna Fáil two out of three in the three-seaters—and also incidentally admitted that he had not seen the bill before it was published—but made it clear that he did not expect this eventuality to occur. 'The Minister for Local Government is not St Francis of Assisi,' he explained.[74]

The second reading debate dragged on for five more days.[75] It was notable for the absence of front-bench participation (except for Fitzpatrick who tried to argue his way out of his previous advocacy of an independent commission) and for the profusion of Fianna Fáil speakers.

Meanwhile there had been considerable adverse reaction from local papers in the south and west. The Cork *Evening Echo*, a paper long sympathetic to Fine Gael, incensed by the removal of 10,000 suburban Cork voters from the new five-seat Cork City constituency and their transfer to a sprawling Mid-Cork which extended as far as the Kerry borders, trumpeted 'Will Cork City Accept this Treatment?' and urged the Minister and parliamentary secretary, who were among the city deputies, to rectify this 'downgrading'[76]—but to no avail.

To all the Fianna Fáil arguments the government deputies could only reply at the *tu quoque* level. This was also true of Tully's reply to the whole debate on 11 December.[77] He made no attempt to rebut any of the detailed charges, but devoted most of his speech to an exposition of the bill that Molloy had allegedly been preparing—which he had found on taking over the department—and which would have been even worse! (Molloy strenuously denied that he had drawn up proposals when in office, only 'exercises'.) To the argument for a commission which Molloy had proposed, Tully gave the same reply as Boland in 1969: 'Apparently the Constitution as at present laid out did not allow a Commission'.[78] The second stage passed amid violent recriminations from both sides of the House.

The committee stage dragged on through February and March until a guillotine motion was introduced on 2 April—by then the debate had lasted fifty-eight hours, compared with forty-eight in 1968-9—and all the remaining stages were taken on that day. It quickly passed through the Senate and became law on 7 May 1974.

The Electoral (Amendment) Act, 1974, or the 'Tullymander', as it became popularly known—the term was in use as early as November 1973—has merited such detailed treatment because of the profound impact it had on the thinking of political commentators right up to polling day in 1977. Their virtually unanimous opinion could be summed up in the words of Peter Mair:

In theory, and given more or less the same voting distribution as in 1973, the Coalition parties could increase their representation in Dublin City from fourteen to eighteen seats, with a corresponding reduction in the Fianna Fáil representation from thirteen seats to nine. This result is made possible through the changed constituency configuration *and does not depend on even one voter changing his or her electoral alleg-iance.*[79] (Author's italics).

(b) In spite of the worsening economic situation, the Coalition parties fared well in by-elections during their four years in office. Their first victory (November 1973) occurred when the Electoral Amendment Bill was going through—a seat won by Fine Gael from Fianna Fáil in Monaghan, following Childers' election to the Presidency. In 1975, following the death of a Fine Gael deputy for West Mayo (where the party had secured 49.4 per cent first preferences in 1973) his son won the by-election with a massive swing of 8 per cent against Fianna Fáil. The deaths of Noel Lemass (son of Sean Lemass) in 1976, and of another Fianna Fáil deputy in Donegal North-East, were followed by the return of a Blaneyite[80] and of the general secretary of the Labour Party—a net loss of two seats to Fianna Fáil. These were the last by-elections to the Twentieth Dáil.

(c) As 1977 approached it was generally accepted that the dissolution would occur in that year; the habit of four-years Dáils now seemed too ingrained to alter. In January, the Minister for Finance introduced a popular budget which was in marked contrast to his draconian budgets of the previous years. This was taken as an indication that the dissolution would be in June rather than October—the two most likely months for fighting elections. However, the Taoiseach kept his own counsel, and it was not until the Fine Gael Ard Fheis, at the weekend of 21-22 May, that Cosgrave revealed the proximity of the election in a vehement speech attacking irresponsible commentators ('blow-ins', he called them) and civil rights agitators who were 'vilifying' the Minister for Justice and the gardai. This was taken to mean that 'strong government' would be one of the themes of the election.[81] Three days later the Dáil was dissolved by a proclamation of the President, in the presence of a 'relaxed and smiling' Taoiseach, who told newsmen he did not expect any one issue to dominate the campaign.[82]

An incumbent government can normally expect to derive some electoral advantage from its ability to choose the timing of a general election. In 1977, however, this did not happen, for Fianna Fáil produced its election manifesto on the very first day of the campaign (26 May) and it was sufficiently imaginative to ensure that the opposition programme rather than the government one determined the character of the campaign. Fianna Fáil had learnt from their mistakes of 1973. In the intervening years they had radically changed their headquarters organisation, with a youthful general secretary and a full-time press officer and research department. Moreover, Lynch had managed to persuade the previous Ard Fheis to allow the leader to nominate one candidate in every constituency, thus giving the party a wider range of candidate potential than in the past. Fianna Fáil's traditional lack of academic personnel in its ranks was rectified by the presence on its team of Professor Martin O'Donoghue, an economist from Trinity College, Dublin, who for several years had been the party's chief economic adviser. In the words of the editor of *Hibernia* (not noted for a bias in its favour), of the three parties, Fianna Fáil entered the election in the best organisational shape.[83]

The Fianna Fáil manifesto, entitled 'Action Plan for National Reconstruction', concentrated on three major issues: prices, unemployment and youth. It pledged the creation of 20,000 new jobs per annum (5,000 for school-leavers) and grants for new householders, and for the middle class it offered tempting incentives—the abolition of rates on dwelling houses from the beginning of 1978, the abolition of road tax and increased tax allowances. The cost, the party estimated, would be £250 million.

The publication of the Fianna Fáil manifesto effectively stole the Coalition's thunder. The press conference called to expound their manifesto on the following day (27 May) was largely devoted to angry claims that the cost of the Fianna Fáil programme had been greatly underestimated, and that it would bankrupt the country. The Coalition programme promised little more than a National Development Corporation to tackle the unemployment problem, and the gradual abolition of rates over a two-year period. The leaders explained that they were going into the election on their record, and disdained to conduct an 'auction' with Fianna Fáil. A similar attitude was displayed the following day, when Lynch issued a challenge to Cosgrave to a television debate which the Taoiseach spurned ('I will not descend into the market place').

That same day, Cosgrave gave an indication of the issues he regarded as most relevant—firmness and determination in government. Three days later Cruise O'Brien and John Kelly both attacked the past inconsistencies of Fianna Fáil policy on Northern Ireland and in an interview on the BBC O'Brien attacked Haughey as a 'dangerous force'.

Fianna Fáil replied that this was a smear campaign, designed to divert the voters' attention from the real (economic) issues, and the *Irish Times* warned the Coalition that such tactics could lose them votes.[84] The security issue and Northern Ireland were scarcely raised in the campaign thereafter.

Another tactical advantage secured by Fianna Fáil was the launching of a nationwide speaking tour by Lynch, during which he visited all but three constituencies. It was like the 'Let's Back Jack' campaign of 1969, only more so. Although he had not been prominent in the Dáil during the previous year, having been ill, and was constantly having his imminent retirement predicted, Lynch indulged in a presidential-style campaign reminiscent of de Valera. The other party front-benchers generally confined themselves to their constituencies. Fine Gael's reaction was uncertain. Cosgrave did not start his speaking tour until 1 June, with unheralded appearances in Sligo and Mayo; then back to Dublin, then Offaly, then at the beginning of the last crucial week he contracted laryngitis. Corish's campaign was also sporadic.

Whereas Fianna Fáil had been rent by internal strife in 1973, it was now Labour's turn. The deputies who had opposed the emergency legislation were welcomed back to the fold; but a line was drawn at Dr Noel Browne, whom the party association in Dublin (Artane) wished to nominate, and at his colleague from the Liaison of the Left, Matt Merrigan. When the Administrative Council (the party's national executive) refused to confirm their candidatures they stood as Independent Labour. Trouble was also caused by the imposition of two new candidates in other Dublin constituencies. Labour played a low-key role in this campaign; they had no separate manifesto or press conference, and of the leaders, only Corish and O'Brien made much impact.

Seventy-one Independents and others were nominated as against fifty in 1973. They included two communists and a few from varying branches of socialism. Official Sinn Féin, now renamed Sinn Féin-the Workers' Party, produced sixteen candidates and a fully socialist programme. They had had some respectable polls in the 1974 local elections and to quote their leader, Tomás Mac Giolla, they hoped to establish 'a basis for further seats next time'.[85] In Dublin six 'Community' candidates stood; they were solely concerned with the problems of the sprawling capital.

That Fianna Fáil were making the running appeared evident in the last week of the campaign when Fine Gael spokesmen were on the defensive about unemployment figures—Lynch claimed that the true figure was 180,000,[86] FitzGerald adhered to the official figure of 111,000 and Cosgrave refused to discuss statistics—and this impression was reinforced when, on 9 June, the Coalition published a 'Greater Dublin Plan' (40,000 new houses, more jobs for young people, a flat dwellers' charter, measures against vandalism and a Dublin Transport Authority). All these amenities, the Minister for Finance claimed, could be provided within the existing expenditure projections.[87] (It must be mentioned that the Coalition programme was not costed.) The last days of the campaign were marked by Fianna Fáil charges that the government was deliberately suppressing recommendations by the National Prices Commission for price increases on a wide range of essential goods—and heated ministerial denials. On the eve of polling day (15 June), newspapers carried a full-page message from Jack Lynch, 'To the People of Ireland', urging them to support the Fianna Fáil programme, 'a good plan, carefully researched and costed', not a detail of which had had to be changed in spite of all the Coalition criticisms. Fine Gael also presented a full-page advertisement, showing a large photograph of Cosgrave and smaller ones of the nine Fine Gael ministers ('The Team you Can Trust') and urging the voters to vote Fine Gael. Labour issued no separate advertisement, but there was a joint message urging supporters of both parties to vote the Coalition ticket. (For the first time none of the three parties held an eve-of-poll rally in Dublin.)

The newspapers' treatment of the campaign was interesting. No previous election had received such saturation press coverage, in addition to continual commentaries on radio and television. Each Dublin daily had a team of reporters following the course of the campaign through the country, and providing 'constituency profiles' for the benefit of their readers, as well as articles by their regular political correspondents. At the beginning of the campaign, the prevailing sentiment was expressed in the *Irish Press* by Michael Mills, who soberly assessed the effects of the 'Tully Carve-Up'— two seats lost to Fianna Fáil in Cavan-Monaghan and Donegal, and possibly two more in Dublin, without a single vote changing hands (27 May). At the mid-point there was also general agreement that while Fianna Fáil had narrowed the gap, it still had a long way to go. The 'Dublin Package' was also thought to be a sign that the Coalition felt vulnerable in the capital.

Nevertheless, the final assessments gave no hint that the correspondents knew what was coming. On 13 June, when Lynch predicted that Fianna Fáil would win seventy-seven seats, the *Irish Press* analysts made it clear that they did not believe him; such a victory would require a swing of between 4 per cent and 5 per cent in some constituencies (14 June). On the morning after polling day, before the votes were counted, Mills concluded that it was 'highly probable' that the result would be determined 'not by manifestos or credibility, but by the re-drawing of constituencies' (17 June). The *Irish Independent* did not make a definite prediction. Their leading political correspondent, Bruce Arnold, throughout the campaign poured scorn on both groups for not facing up to the real issues—unemployment figures, he predicted, might be as high as 300,000 by 1981—and lashed the Coalition rather more than Fianna Fáil.[88] Mid-way, he admitted that Fianna Fáil had redressed the bias against them at the beginning of the campaign; but the 'key question' was whether they could overcome the 'devastating gerrymander' (4 June).

The *Irish Times* not only dispatched a team of reporters to the various constituencies but also commissioned NOP to conduct three opinion polls during the campaign.[89] The pollsters did not ask the direct question of how people intended to vote, but sought an assessment of the parties on various grounds. They found that on economic issues Fianna Fáil was well ahead (25 per cent), but on social issues, security and Northern Ireland the Coalition had a narrow lead. When asked what politician would make the best Taoiseach, assuming a Fianna Fáil/Coalition victory, 73 per cent opted for Lynch and only 44 per cent for Cosgrave. These findings, like those of the earlier IMS surveys, were not fully appreciated, even by the *Irish Times*. On polling day (16 June), a collation of last-minute reports from their constituency correspondents produced the following predictions: Fianna Fáil, sixty-three to seventy-one seats ('their maximum possible'); Fine Gael, fifty-three to sixty seats; Labour, twenty-one to twenty-four seats; while the chief political correspondent of the *Times* predicted that 'Fianna Fáil will be doing well to win seventy seats; Fine Gael seem set to take fifty-seven. Labour may drop one or two, possibly ending up with nineteen'. The fortnightly *Hibernia,* in its first issue of the campaign (27 May), boldly predicted on its front page; Fianna Fáil, sixty-eight; Fine

Gael, fifty-eight, Labour, twenty. In the next issue it slightly modified these predictions, giving Fianna Fáil an extra seat (10 June). (When the actual results came in only one correspondent of any newspaper donned the appropriate sackcloth!)[90]

Editorially, the *Irish Press,* as always, staunchly supported Fianna Fáil. The *Independent,* while professing impartiality, gave the Coalition somewhat muted support: on polling day the editor (unlike his political correspondent) found it 'impossible to escape the conclusion' that the Coalition should be given a fresh mandate.

The *Irish Times* editorially assumed an air of almost olympian detachment. At the outset, the editor warned the Coalition that 'gerrymanders have been known to work against their authors', and deprecated their tentendency to blame all economic difficulties on external factors. There was plenty of evidence of 'lack of coherence and drive' on the part of the government. On the other hand, the editor averred that it would take more than Martin O'Donoghue to remove from Fianna Fáil the image of 'yesterday's men' (26 May). At the mid-point of the campaign the editor posed the question whether Fianna Fáil would have been able to handle the economic problems better than the Coalition and answered, 'probably no better, or possibly slightly worse' (8 June).

On the day before polling the editor still regarded Fianna Fáil as a 'tired old team' that would benefit from 'a few more years of reconstruction, out of office'; but also expressed disillusionment with the government's performance. In 1973, he wrote, the formation of the Coalition had held out a hope for the emergence of a progressive social democracy, but the reality had been different. Cosgrave was dominant, Costello out of politics,[91] and FitzGerald 'a one-man liberal wing of his party'. The best result, in the editorial opinion, would be an increased vote for Labour and a diminished Fine Gael vote (15 June).

This was the first election in which the age group eighteen to twenty-one was eligible to vote, and first-time voters constituted a staggering 25 per cent of the total electorate of 2.1 million. Thus, although the turnout was slightly down on 1973—from 76.6 per cent to 76.3 per cent—the total number of valid was 1.6 million—the highest ever. Counting began on the morning of Friday 17 June, and within a few hours of the first results being declared the Taoiseach had conceded defeat. There was no doubting the magnitude of the Fianna Fáil victory. Fianna Fáil secured 50.6 per cent of the first preferences (an increase of 4.4 per cent); Fine Gael, 30.5 per cent (a loss of 4.6 per cent); Labour, 11.6 per cent (a loss of 2.1 per cent). Sinn Féin increased from 1.1 per cent to 1.7 per cent, and Independents and others went up from 3 per cent to 5.6 per cent, their best performance since 1961.

Thus Fianna Fáil won an overall majority of the national vote—an extremely rare achievement in democracies, comparable with the achievement of the British Conservatives in 1931 and 1935, the Greek Rally in

90

1952, the Greek New Democracy in 1974, the West German Christian Democrats in 1957, the Swedish Social Democrats in 1968, and, of course, Fianna Fáil itself in 1938. It won eighty-four seats (an increase of sixteen); Fine Gael dropped from fifty-four seats to forty-three, and Labour from nineteen to sixteen. Four Independents were returned: Noel Browne and a candidate from Limerick, both standing as Independent Labour against official Labour nominees; Blaney again as Independent Fianna Fáil, and Joseph Sheridan, who had been returned as an Independent for Longford-Westmeath at every election since 1961.

Fianna Fáil secured a greater premium of seats than in 1938 and seven more seats than even Lynch (the most optimistic forecaster) had predicted. Its success seems to have been enhanced rather than mitigated by the constituency revision. In five 5-seaters it won three out of five seats; in eighteen out of twenty-six 3-seaters it won two out of three; and, most remarkable of all, in three 4-seaters (Galway East, Galway West and Louth) it won three out of four seats. (Even in 1938 and 1957 Fianna Fáil never scored such a victory in more than one 4-seater.) In twenty-two out of forty-two constituencies Fianna Fáil secured over 50 per cent of first preferences—the comparable figures for 1969 and 1973 were thirteen and sixteen respectively—and in seven others secured over 48 per cent. Its highest poll was 68.9 per cent in the three-seat constituency, Clare. The swing, though varying, extended through the country. In the Dublin constituencies Fianna Fáil achieved less than 40 per cent in two; 40 per cent to 50 per cent in eight, and over 50 per cent in four; it won twenty-three of forty-three seats.

Among those who lost their seats were two Labour Ministers, Justin Keating (Industry and Commerce) and Conor Cruise O'Brien (Posts and Telegraphs), and the Fine Gael Minister for Justice, Patrick Cooney. Other casualties were David Thornley and the general secretary of the Labour Party, Brendan Halligan. To the glee of political correspondents, James Tully only got in at the last count in his Meath constituency.

The Coalition defeat was enhanced by the performance of dissident Labour candidates in Dublin and Limerick, by Community candidates in Dublin, all of whom polled respectably (including the irrepressible Mr Loftus, now calling himself 'Sean Dublin Bay Loftus', who went as far as the second last count in Clontarf), and by transfers to Fianna Fáil from Sinn Féin and Independents. (The question of the distribution of transfers from Fine Gael and Labour will be discussed in Chapter 9.) With more candidates than in 1973, Sinn Féin fared somewhat better in votes, but nowhere came close to winning a seat.

What was the cause of such a complete and unexpected electoral reverse? The newspapers were full of *post factum* explanations. The landslide was an expression of popular revulsion against repressive government; it was due to Lynch's presidential-style campaign; it was a reaction against Cosgrave's uninspiring leadership; it was caused by the failure of the Coalition to cope with the really important issues of prices and unemployment, and/or to organise their campaign efficiently. In an article in the *Irish Times* (21 June), FitzGerald admitted that the government had not paid sufficient attention to manifestations of discontent in the opinion polls, and also suggested that a possible source of the massive Fianna Fáil vote was the youngest segment of the electorate.[92] Perhaps the most frank comment of all was in the *Irish Independent* editorial on the morning after the landslide:

> It was a rout. There is no point in looking for euphemistic terms. The swing was greater than political commentators had forecast, was even bigger than Fianna Fáil had anticipated ... [it]can only be described as a devastating display of public displeasure. (18 June)

Within a week of the election, Cosgrave announced his resignation from the Fine Gael leadership; and Corish, who had signified his intention before the election, resigned the leadership of Labour. To replace them, the Labour Party elected Frank Cluskey (a Dublin trade unionist who had been a deputy since 1965 and was a parliamentary secretary in the Coalition) by a one-vote majority over Michael O'Leary, a Cork-born former research officer for the ITGWU who was the outgoing Minister for Labour; while Fine Gael had an uncontested election, Garret FitzGerald being elevated to the leadership just eight years after entering the Dáil.

When the Twenty-first Dáil met, on 5 July, the deputy leader of Fianna Fáil, Joseph Brennan, was elected Ceann Comhairle in a contest with the outgoing Ceann Comhairle, Sean Treacy. (Treacy's defeat meant that the total of Labour deputies was raised to seventeen.) Jack Lynch was elected Taoiseach and set about forming his third administration, with Colley as Tanaiste and Haughey as Minister for Health. At his first press conference after resuming office, Lynch promised to introduce legislation entrusting the revision of constituencies to an independent commission.

8
The Irish Parties and the Party System

I
THE PARTIES' SOCIAL BASES

Writing in 1933, Warner Moss stated that Cumann na nGaedheal was the party of the local business leaders, the older priests, and the prosperous farmers; while Fianna Fáil was supported by the lower middle class groups and many who, though not in the Labour Party, were anxious for social reform.[1] Many years later, McCracken pointed out that the anti-Treaty party had originally relied chiefly on the small farmers, shopkeepers and sections of the artisan and labouring classes but had progressively broadened its appeal; while Labour had suffered not only from the paucity of the urban industrial population, but from its failure to capture the full support of the class, small though it was.[2]

Apart from analysing the occupations of Dáil deputies (as McCracken did) these authors had to rely on general impressions of the social bases of the parties. Survey evidence, the raw material of political sociology, did not become available until much later in Ireland. The earliest survey of political attitudes was a poll on the EEC entry issue organised by the *Irish Press* in July 1961. The first detailed survey of party support was undertaken by Gallup Polls (Dublin) in April 1969. The most recent survey, conducted by Irish Marketing Surveys, was commissioned by Radio Telefís Eireann in September 1976.

The Gallup survey was extensively analysed by John H. Whyte in his lengthy article, 'Ireland: Politics without social bases' in *Electoral Behaviour: A Comparative Handbook,* edited by Richard Rose, London 1974, 619-53. By kind permission of Dr Whyte and Radio Telefís Eireann I reproduce in the following tables the relevant data from the two surveys concerning party support correlated with class, region and age group. The design of both surveys was similar: Gallup (Weighted N = 1,580, interviewed N = 2,135, owing to fuller sampling of the Dublin area); IMS (Weighted N = 2,038, interviewed N = 1,004). Gallup used six class categories:

AB—upper and middle-class; higher and intermediate managers, administrators and proprietors;

C1—lower middle-class; clerical staff and junior managers, administrators and proprietors;

C2—skilled manual workers;

DE—unskilled manual workers, labourers, pensioners;

F1—farmers with more than thirty acres;

F2—farmers with less than thirty acres.

IMS used an almost identical classification, except that F1 contains farmers with more than fifty acres, and F2 includes farm labourers (coded as manual workers by Gallup). All figures given in percentages.

PARTY AND CLASS

1969

	FF	FG	Lab.	Other†
AB	37	37	10	17
C1	48	26	15	11
C2	40	21	27	12
DE	43	14	28	15
F1	38	46	2	14
F2	53	26	5	16
All classes (100%)	43	25	18	14

1976

	FF	FG	Lab.	Coalition*	Other†
AB	27	32	13	6	22
C1	39	19	18	3	22
C2	45	16	14	2	22
DE	45	14	22	3	16
F1	38	46	4	—	11
F2	47	33	7	4	9
All classes (100%)	43	23	15	3	17

*The IMS survey asked voters whether they supported the 'Coalition' as well as an individual party.
†Including 'Don't knows' and 'None'.

PARTY AND REGION

1969

	FF	FG	Lab.	Other
Dublin	36	20	26	17
Connacht/ Ulster	47	28	9	16
Rest of Leinster	42	28	20	10
Munster	46	25	16	13

1976

	FF	FG	Lab.	Coalition	Other
Dublin	39	15	23	5	19
Connacht/ Ulster	51	34	1	1	14
Rest of Leinster	36	25	16	5	18
Munster	46	20	16	1	18

PARTY AND AGE GROUP

1969

	FF	FG	Lab.	Other
21-4*	34	22	28	15
24-34	43	24	22	12
35-44	42	27	17	15
45-54	41	25	20	14
55-64	52	22	14	12
65+	43	28	12	16

1976

	FF	FG	Lab.	Coalition	Other
21-4*	40	16	20	2	22
25-34	41	17	19	2	21
35-44	48	25	10	2	15
45-54	45	28	11	4	12
55-64	47	23	12	5	13
65+	38	28	15	3	15

*In the 1976 survey this category was '18-24'

Summing up his lengthy analysis of the 1969 survey, Dr Whyte concluded that Irish electoral behaviour was 'exceptionally unstructured' (p. 645), and that the social influences affecting party development in other countries were much less significant in Ireland. In the comparative table covering the western democracies presented by Richard Rose in the same volume Ireland was placed away at the end of the field—the percentage variance figure for the three main factors (occupation, religion and region) was 3.1 in the case of Ireland, whereas the average percentage was 26.7 (p. 17).

The data furnished by the 1976 survey do not materially alter this conclusion. Changes in individual percentages should not be overstressed on account of the small numbers involved in the sets and the statistical margin of error. With these reservations one may advert to the following shifts suggested by the 1976 survey: (1) an increase in the 'don't knows', suggesting greater voting mobility;[3] (2) an increase in the Fianna Fáil share of support from the youngest age group, and (3) a decline of Fianna Fáil support in the upper and middle classes, while its capacity to attract working class support remained unimpaired.

In general, then, one might say that Fianna Fáil is still, as it has been since the late 1930s, a 'catchall' party with a heterogeneous social base; that Fine Gael (though much less successful) is also heterogeneous, and that Labour is at the other end of the scale, a party whose main support comes from sections of one class.

II
THE IRISH PARTY SYSTEM

In 1954, in his classic, *Political Parties*,[4] Maurice Duverger made the first attempt to construct a theory of party systems. He found that democratic political systems fell into one of two categories, two-party or multi-party, depending on the character of the electoral system—the majority system sustaining the 'natural' tendency to party dualism, while PR tended to a proliferation of parties, through splits in existing parties and the formation of new ones.

Duverger's book was concerned not only with systems analysis but all aspects of party; while its shortcomings have been recognised it spawned two major types of research. On the one hand were the writings of political sociologists, less interested in electoral mechanisms than in social influences on party and voter, who produced theories of party *development*. Among the names that may be mentioned are Epstein, La Palombara, Weiner, Henig and Pinder;[5] but possibly the most celebrated theory is that adumbrated by Lipset and Rokkan.[6] These authors argue that democratic party systems have developed in accordance with four different kinds of cleavage, corresponding to four crucial junctures in the history of Western nation-states: conflicts between centre and periphery (from the Reformation and Counter-Reformation), between Church and state (from the French Revolution), between land and industry (from the Industrial Revolution), and between workers and employers (from the Russian Revolution). Three of these cleavages clearly have little relevance to Irish conditions, but Tom Garvin has made a strong case for the relevance of the centre-periphery cleavage—Fianna Fáil being originally concentrated in the western counties and gradually extending eastwards until by 1938 it was the largest party in almost every constituency.[7]

Other scholars at the level of micro-politics have argued that in some (especially rural) constituencies, some (especially Fianna Fáil) politicians maintain a clientelistic relationship with their constituents, the TD being cast in the role of a provider of benefits and services (e.g. Chubb, Bax and Sacks).[8]

The other major concern of students of party has been with party systems. In 1969 Jean Blondel produced another model in *An Introduction to Comparative Government.* He pointed out that to define party systems in terms of the number of parties securing representation was insufficient, since relative strength is also critical. ('A four-party system* in which one is equal to the other three together is different from one in which all parties have about equal strength'—p. 138). Examining the election returns in some twenty western democracies in the period 1945-66, and concentrating on the share of the vote secured by the *two* largest parties as the most important variable, Blondel was able to distinguish four categories: (1) where the average vote of the two major parties exceeded 90 per cent; (2) where it ranged between 75 per cent and 80 per cent; (3) where it fell between 62 per cent and 66 per cent, and (4) where it was 50 per cent or less. These Blondel calls respectively two-party systems (e.g. the USA); two-and-a-half party systems (e.g. West Germany); multi-party systems with a dominant party (e.g. Sweden), and multi-party systems without a dominant party (e.g. Switzerland). In examining the second category (West Germany, Belgium, Canada, Ireland and Luxembourg). Blondel found the two largest parties considerably and consistently larger than the third and concluded that three-party systems are inherently unstable.[9]

The latest addition to the literature on party systems is Giovanni Sartori's *Parties and Party Systems,* the first volume of which has already appeared. The Sartori model contains the following categories: multipartism (more than 'five or six' parties); pluralism (where there are four or less significant parties—further subdivided into polarised and moderate pluralism, depending on the presence or absence of 'anti-system' parties), and a predominant-party system, which prevails 'to the extent that, and

---

*It must be remembered that in the literature on party systems the terms 'two-party', 'one-party' are not used literally, but refer to a tendency.

as long as, its major party is consistently supported by a winning majority (the absolute majority of seats) of the voters' (p. 196).

Party systems, like other systems, must exhibit mutual interdependence of parts and clearly defined boundaries. The difficulty with Sartori's model is that he does not draw a consistent line between his categories. For example, in the same chapter Ireland is classified with Luxembourg among the countries 'which hardly lend themselves to dispute as cases of limited and moderate pluralism' (p. 182), and also as falling into the 'predominant-party' category between 1932 and 1973, with an interruption from 1948 to 1957 (p. 198). The concept of a 'predominant party' is difficult to operationalise, except where one party consistently wins 50 per cent or more of the seats. Northern Ireland, 1922-69, is the only such case, and it is normally excluded from comparative studies of party since it was not a sovereign state—as Sartori concedes in referring to 'the relatively high rate of entries and exits' from this category (p. 201).

With Blondel's model, on the other hand, the lines of division are too tightly drawn. Within each of his clusters, 'if we exclude the United States, which is at the very top in this classification, no country is nearer to any country outside its own group than it is to all the other countries within its group' (p. 156). But this result is conditioned by the empirical data on which he worked. Since 1968 Belgium has gradually moved into the multiparty category. And what of the Irish elections of 1927 (September), 1944, 1951 and 1957, when the two largest parties secured less than 75 per cent (the lower limit of the two-and-a-half party group in Blondel's table) and more than 66 per cent (the top of the multi-party group)? These variations suggest that when a model of party systems is being constructed the boundary between one category and another should not be too rigid.

The evidence would suggest that the necessary elements in a theory of party systems are the number of parties winning seats in the legislature and their relative position. (Voting figures are, as we have seen, subject to distortion by the electoral system.) A more elaborate model would incorporate other variables—ideological and organisational differences and the nature of support in the electorate—although, as the Irish experience has shown, these variables may not always be of great significance.

Taking the first two variables into account one may classify party systems as follows:

1. Where two parties secure 90 per cent or more of the seats there is a two-party system.

2. Where three parties secure 90 per cent or more of the seats there is a three-party system. (In the special case where the third party has less than half the seats won by the second it may be called a two-and-a-half party system.)

3. All other cases involving four or more parties constitute multiparty systems.

It will be noted that this typology excludes the case where *one* party consistently gets 50 per cent of the seats. This is both politically and statistically highly improbable and can occur only in cases where ordinary political divisions are cross-cut by a deeper cleavage (as in Northern Ireland).

The next question to be asked is how long must one of these combinations persist before a particular country can be claimed for a particular party system? Variations will obviously occur from election to election and nobody would claim that *one* election result could establish a party system. Here unfortunately no measure can be chosen which is not arbitrary. Sartori suggests as a 'sensible' answer, four consecutive results at least (p. 196), and I would tend to agree.

Armed with these simple analytical tools we can say that between 1923 and 1957 a multi-party system prevailed in Ireland, evolving from 1961 into a two-and-a-half party system. If in future elections the gap between Fine Gael and Labour should narrow a three-party system might emerge. Blondel argues that third parties are either coming or going, but he has not shown that this *must* be so.

In the multi-party period the only divergent Irish results were those of 1937 (when the distribution of seats corresponded to a three-party system) and 1938 (when it approximated to a two-party system). But by 1943 multi-partism was re-established. 1954 also resembled 1937.

What effects may be predicted of party systems? Subsequent research has not modified Duverger's contention that a two-party system produces 'majority-bent' parties with an eye to power, with a consequent facility in forming governments, while multi-party systems tend to promote 'minority-bent' parties, with short-term rather than long-term objectives and less concern for the formation of stable governments, and in consequence Cabinet crises are more frequent and more intractable. A two-and-a-half party system (as the Irish experience over the past seventeen years has shown) is closer to the first than the second of these types.

9

Proportionality in Irish Elections

When first studying Irish elections, more than twenty years ago, I noted that previous authors, when dealing with results, used to reproduce in parallel columns the figures for 'seats obtained' and 'seats in proportion to votes' for each party concerned. This was too imprecise to measure deviations from proportionality, especially when comparing elections in which there were variations in the total number of seats, so I worked out each figure in the first column mentioned above as a percentage of the corresponding figure in the second column, and called the result the 'index of proportionality', full proportionality being represented by the figure 100.[1]

The index of proportionality has been found useful by other students of elections in the Republic, but it has its limitations. It takes account only of *national* totals, irrespective of the number of candidates involved; so in the case of a small party putting up just a few candidates in constituencies where it is believed to have a good chance of securing the election of most of them—perhaps helped by transfers from larger parties—the index can be misleading. (See, for example, the very high indices for Independent Republicans in June 1927, Farmers in 1932 and Clann na Talmhan in 1951.) In the case of parties that contest all, or almost all, constituencies the index is most reliable.

In presenting the results of the elections from 1923 to 1977 inclusive, I have calculated the index of proportionality by dividing a party's share of the seats by its share of the votes, using a base of 100. But I also provide for each general election a figure, derived from the well-known analytical study by Douglas Rae, *The Political Consequences of Electoral Laws*, which is probably the best overall measure of proportionality, the 'average vote-seat deviation'. This is calculated by subtracting the share of the seats obtained by each party in an election from its share of the votes, aggregating the results, and dividing by the number of competing parties. (Rae excludes from his survey parties securing less than 0.5 per cent of the national vote, so all such groups are classified with 'Independents' in the following tables.)[2] For the reader's convenience the indices of proportionality of Fianna Fáil (Sinn Féin in 1923), Cumann na nGaedheal/Fine Gael and Labour are reproduced in the accompanying graph.

100

The index of proportionality (in the seventh column) gives the deviation from proportionality in the case of each party. Thus, any figure above 100 means that the party secured more seats in the whole country than it deserved proportionally, while a figure below 100 means that it secured fewer seats. The average vote-seat deviation is an average figure for the whole election, 2.1 per cent in 1923 meaning that on average each party's share of the seats deviated by 2.1 per cent from its share of the votes in that general election.

IRISH GENERAL ELECTIONS (1923-77)

Year	Party	% of Vote	Seats won	% of Seats	Seats in Proportion to Votes	Index of Proportion-ality
1923	C na G	39.0	63	42.0	59	108
	Sinn Féin	27.4	44	29.3	41	107
	Lab.	10.6	14	9.3	16	88
	Far.	12.1	15	10.0	18	83
	Ind.	10.9	14(+3)	9.3	16	85
	Total	100.0	150(+3)	100.0	150(+3)	—

Turnout: 59% Average vote/seat deviation: 2.1%

Year	Party	% of Vote	Seats won	% of Seats	Seats in Proportion to Votes	Index of Proportion-ality
1927 (June)	C na G	27.4	46	30.3	42	111
	FF	26.1	44	28.9	40	111
	Lab.	12.6	22	14.5	19	115
	Far.	8.9	11	7.2	14	81
	Nat. Leag.	7.3	8	5.3	11	73
	Sinn Féin	3.6	5	3.3	5	92
	Ind. Reps.	0.8	2	1.3	1	162
	Clann Eir.	0.5	—	—	1	—
	Ind.	12.8	14	9.2	19	72
	Total	100.0	152	100.0	152	—

Turnout: 66.4% Average vote/seat deviation: 1.6%

Year	Party	% of Vote	Seats won	% of Seats	Seats in Proportion to Votes	Index of Proportion-ality
1927 (Sept.)	C na G	38.7	61	40.9	58	106
	FF	35.2	57	38.3	52	109
	Lab.	9.1	13	8.7	14	96
	Far.	6.4	6	4.0	9	62
	Nat. Leag.	1.6	2	1.3	2	81
	Comm.	1.1	1	0.7	2	64
	Ind.	8.0	9(+3)	6.0	12	75
	Total	100.0	149(+3)	100.0	149(+3)	—

Turnout: 67.9% Average vote/seat deviation: 1.5%

Year	Party	% of Vote	Seats won	% of Seats	Seats in Proportion to Votes	Index of Proportion-ality
1932	FF	44.5	72	48.3	66	109
	C na G	35.3	56	37.6	53	107
	Lab.	7.7	7	4.7	11	61
	Far.	2.1	5	3.4	3	162
	Ind.	10.5	9(+3)	6.0	16	57
	Total	100.0	149(+3)	100.0	149(+3)	–

Turnout: 75.3%. Average vote/seat deviation: 2.6%

Year	Party	% of Vote	Seats won	% of Seats	Seats in Proportion to Votes	Index of Proportion-ality
1933	FF	49.7	76	51.0	74	103
	C na G	30.5	48	32.2	45	106
	Centre	9.1	11	7.4	14	81
	Lab.	5.7	8	5.4	8	95
	Ind.	5.0	6(+3)	4.0	8	80
	Total	100.0	149(+3)	100.0	149(+3)	–

Turnout: 80.4%. Average vote/seat deviation: 1.25%

Year	Party	% of Vote	Seats won	% of Seats	Seats in Proportion to Votes	Index of Proportion-ality
1937	FF	45.2	68	49.6	62	110
	FG	34.8	48	35.0	48	101
	Lab.	10.3	13	9.5	14	92
	Ind.	9.7	8	5.8	13	60
	Total	100.0	137	100.0	137	–

Turnout: 74.6%. Average vote/seat deviation: 1.8%

Year	Party	% of Vote	Seats won	% of Seats	Seats in Proportion to Votes	Index of Proportion-ality
1938	FF	51.9	72(+4)	55.0	68	106
	FG	33.3	43(+2)	32.8	44	98
	Lab.	10.0	9	6.9	13	69
	Ind.	4.7	7	5.3	6	113
	Total	100.0	131(+6)	100.0	131(+6)	–

Turnout: 75.8. Average vote/seat deviation: 2.2%

Year	Party	% of Vote	Seats won	% of Seats	Seats in Proportion to Votes	Index of Proportion-ality
1943	FF	41.9	66	48.2	57	115
	FG	23.1	32	23.4	32	101
	Lab.	15.7	17	12.4	22	79
	C na T	10.3	13	9.5	14	92
	Ind	9.0	9	6.6	12	73
	Total	100.0	137	100.0	137	--

Turnour: 73.3%. Average vote/seat deviation 2.7%

Year	Party	% of Vote	Seats won	% of Seats	Seats in Proportion to Votes	Index of Proportion- ality
1944	FF	48.9	73(+2)	54.5	66	111
	FG	20.5	29(+1)	21.6	27	105
	C na T	10.8	11	8.2	14	76
	Lab.	8.8	8	6.0	12	68
	Nat. Lab.	2.7	4	3.0	4	111
	Ind.	8.4	9	6.7	11	80
	Total	100.0	134(+3)	100.0	134(+3)	—

Turnout: 68.5%. Average vote/seat deviation: 2.5%

Year	Party	% of Vote	Seats won	% of Seats	Seats in Proportion to Votes	Index of Proportion- ality
1948	FF	41.9	67	45.9	61	110
	FG	19.8	31	21.2	29	107
	Lab.	8.7	14	9.6	13	110
	C na P	13.2	10	6.8	19	52
	C na T	5.3	7	4.8	8	91
	Nat. Lab.	2.6	5	3.4	4	131
	Ind.	8.5	12	8.2	12	96
	Total	100.0	146	100.0	146	—

Turnout: 73.5%. Average vote/seat deviation: 2.3%

Year	Party	% of Vote	Seats won	% of Seats	Seats in Proportion to Votes	Index of Proportion- ality
1951	FF	46.3	68	46.6	68	101
	FG	25.7	40	27.4	37	107
	Lab.	11.4	16	11.0	17	96
	C na T	2.9	6	4.1	4	141
	C na P	4.1	2	1.4	6	34
	Ind.	9.6	14	9.6	14	100
	Total	100.0	146	100.0	146	—

Turnout: 74.6% Average vote/seat deviation: 1.3%

Year	Party	% of Vote	Seats won	% of Seats	Seats in Proportion to Votes	Index of Proportion- ality
1954	FF	43.4	65	44.5	63	103
	FG	32.0	50	34.2	47	107
	Lab.	12.1	18	12.3	18	102
	C na T	3.1	5	3.4	4	110
	C na P	3.8	3	2.1	6	55
	Ind.	5.7	5	3.4	8	60
	Total	100.0	146	100.0	146	—

Turnout: 75.5%. Average vote/seat deviation: 1.1%

Year	Party	% of Vote	Seats won	% of Seats	Seats in Proportion to Votes	Index of Proportion-ality
1957	FF	48.3	78	53.4	71	111
	FG	26.6	40	27.4	39	103
	Lab.	9.1	11	7.5	13	82
	Sinn Féin	5.3	4	2.7	8	51
	C na T	2.4	3	2.1	3	88
	C na P	1.7	1	0.7	2	41
	Ind.	6.6	9	6.2	10	94
	Total	100.0	146	100.0	146	94

Turnout: 70.6%. Average vote/seat deviation: 1.9%

Year	Party	% of Vote	Seats won	% of Seats	Seats in Proportion to Votes	Index of Proportion-ality
1961	FF	43.8	70	48.9	63	112
	FG	32.0	47	32.9	46	103
	Lab.	11.6	15	10.5	17	91
	C na T	1.5	2	1.4	2	93
	NPD	1.0	2	1.4	1	140
	C na P	1.2	1	0.7	2	58
	SF	3.0	0	0	4	—
	Ind.	5.9	6	4.2	8	71
	Total	100.0	143	100.0	143	—

Turnout: 69.9%. Average vote/seat deviation: 1.6%

Year	Party	% of Vote	Seats won	% of Seats	Seats in Proportion to Votes	Index of Proportion-ality
1965	FF	47.7	72	50.3	68	105
	FG	34.1	47	32.9	49	96
	Lab.	15.4	21	14.7	22	95
	C na P	0.7	1	0.7	1	100
	Ind.	2.1	2	1.4	3	67
	Total	100.0	143	100.0	143	

Turnout: 74.5% Average vote/seat deviation: 1.1%

Year	Party	% of Vote	Seats won	% of Seats	Seats in Proportion to Votes	Index of Proportion-ality
1969	FF	45.7	74	51.7	65	113
	FG	34.1	50	35.0	49	103
	Lab.	17.0	18	12.6	24	74
	Ind.	3.2	1	0.7	5	22
	Total	100.0	143	100.0	143	

Turnout: 76.9% Average vote/seat deviation: 3.8%

Year	Party	% of Vote	Seats Won	% of Seats	Seats in Proportion to votes	Index of Proportion-ality
1973	FF	46.2	68	47.6	66	103
	FG	35.1	54	37.8	50	108
	Lab.	13.7	19	13.3	20	97
	SF	1.1	0	0	2	–
	AE	0.9	0	0	1	–
	Ind.	3.0	2	1.4	4	47
	Total	100.0	143	100.0	143	

Turnout: 76.6% Average vote/seat deviation: 1.3%

Year	Party	% of Vote	Seats Won	% of Seats	Seats in Proportion to votes	Index of Proportion-ality
1977	FF	50.6	84	57.1	74	113
	FG	30.5	43	29.3	45	96
	Lab.	11.6	16	10.9	17	94
	SFWP	1.7	0	0	3	–
	Ind.	5.6	4	2.7	8	48
	Total	100.0	147	100.0	147	

Turnout: 76.3%. Average vote/seat deviation 2.5%

1. For the general elections of 1923 and 1927 (June) the contemporary newspapers are the only sources of electoral information. From 1927 (September) to 1944 inclusive, these sources are supplemented by the relevant editions of W. J. Flynn, *Oireachtas and Saorstat Guide,* which give details of candidates' names, party affiliations and votes. These have been checked and corrected by Brian M. Walker, editor of statistics for *A New History of Ireland* (published by the Royal Irish Academy) in a volume of statistics which has not yet appeared. (I am grateful to Dr Walker for access to his figures.) From 1948 onwards the details of all the counts have been published by the Stationery Office, Dublin. The first volume published in 1953 was entitled *Dáil Eireann. Copies of the Public Notices of the Results of the Elections and of the Transfers of Votes in respect of: (a) General Election, 1948. (b) General Election, 1951. (c) Bye-elections, 1944 to 1952 (inclusive).* Subsequent volumes were entitled *Dáil Eireann. Election Results and Transfer of Votes in General Election (May 1954) for Fifteenth Dáil,* etc.

2. In the tables from June 1927 inclusive the outgoing Ceann Comhairle's seat is excluded. Other uncontested seats are put in brackets in the 'Seats won' column. These were as follows: 1923–three (Dublin University, three independents); 1927 (September)–three (do.); 1932–three (do.); 1933–three (do.); 1938–six (Donegal West, two Fianna Fáil, one Fine Gael; Kerry South, two Fianna Fáil; one Fine Gael); 1944–three (Donegal West, two Fianna Fáil, one Fine Gael).

3. The university voters are consolidated with the rest of the electorate for the general elections, 1923 to 1933 inclusive.

4. The votes cast for Larkin's 'Irish Worker League' in September 1927 are classified as 'communist', since that group was the Irish affiliate to the Communist International.

5. There is considerable difficulty in distinguishing between Clann na Talmhan

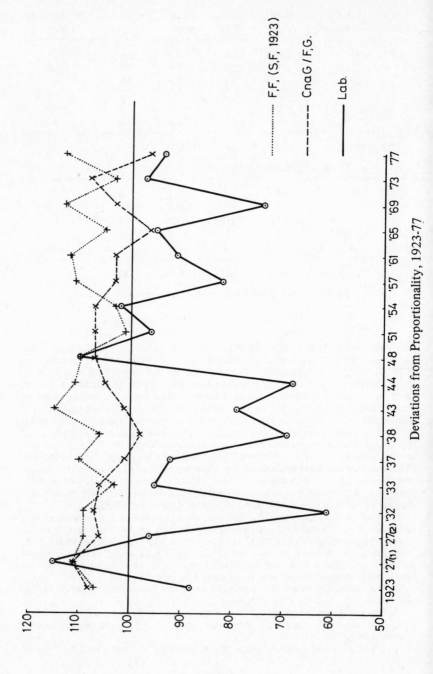

Deviations from Proportionality, 1923-77

F.F. (S.F. 1923)

CnaG / F.G.

Lab.

106

and Independent Farmer candidates in the elections of 1943 and 1944. The contemporary newspapers (very small, owing to newsprint rationing) give conflicting estimates, and the party never possessed a national headquarters, with records etc. These tables are based on the assumption that C na T obtained 137,700 votes and thirteen seats in 1943, and 131,200 votes and eleven seats in 1944.

(a) Overall Deviations from Proportionality

The tables provide interesting, and somewhat surprising results. Over the entire period of fifty-four years and eighteen general elections the largest party (Cumann na nGaedheal in the first three elections, and Fianna Fáil in 1932 and thereafter) secured a premium of seats; the second largest party also has almost always been above the line (the exceptions being 1938, 1965 and 1977); while the Labour party, which took the third highest share of the votes in every election, except 1923, 1933, 1944 and 1948 (when it was beaten into fourth place by Farmers, the Centre Party, Clann na Talmhan and Clann na Poblachta respectively) has consistently secured less seats than it proportionally deserved, except in 1927 (June), 1948 and 1954. (The wide fluctuations in the number of Labour candidates make it difficult to draw firm conclusions about the variations in the party's index of proportionality*.) While the performances of Fianna Fáil and Labour appear to be symmetrical over long stretches (e.g. 1932-44, 1961 onwards), Fine Gael performance has been more irregular; its index of proportionality fell continually from 1932 to 1938, rose until 1948, and then remained steady until 1954, before falling again. (Two of its three indices below 100 fall in the period after 1957). The only elections in which all three parties secured a premium of seats were those in which the greatest number of parties competed (June 1927 and 1948) and also in 1954.

When Rae examined the election results of twenty western democracies (including Ireland) over the twenty-year period from January 1945 to January 1965, he found the average vote-seat deviation to be 1.63 per cent for countries using proportional systems, and 3.96 per cent for majority-type systems. The average for the five Irish elections surveyed by Rae (1948 to 1961 inclusive) was 1.51 per cent† (very close to the average for PR systems generally), but over the whole period 1923-77 it is 1.87 per cent. However, the figures for the five most recent elections are widely divergent. While the average for the period 1961-77 is 1.89 per cent, three figures (1961, 1965 and 1973) are below the average for 1923-57 (1.86 per cent), but the figure for 1969 (3.8 per cent) is the highest ever, and is close to the average for *majority*-type systems in Rae's survey, and the

*The numbers of Labour candidates were as follows: 1923-44; 1927(1)-44; 1927(2)-28; 1932-33; 1933-19; 1937-23; 1938-30; 1943-70; 1944-30; 1948-43; 1951-37; 1954-39; 1957-29; 1961-34; 1965-42; 1969-99; 1973-55; 1977-56.

†If the Ceann Comhairle's seat is excluded (as in this book), the average figure for 1948-61 is 1.6 per cent.

figure for 1977 is the fourth highest. Some explanation must be sought for these wide variations.

(b) Size of Constituencies

Number of Seats	9	8	7	5	4	3	Number of Constituencies	
1923-35	1	3	5	9	4	8	30	(153 seats)
1935-47	–	–	3	8	8	15	34	(138 seats)
1947-61	–	–	–	9	9	22	40	(147 seats)
1961-69	–	–	–	9	12	17	38	(144 seats)
1969-74	–	–	–	2	14	26	42	
1974-	–	–	–	6	10	26	42	(148 seats)

For many years psephologists have claimed that size of constituencies—'district magnitude', as it is called in the United States—is a variable affecting proportionality. In 1945 the late James Hogan wrote: 'The decisive point in PR is the size of the constituencies: the larger the constituency, that is, the greater the number of members which it elects, the more closely will the result approximate to proportionality. On the other hand, the smaller the constituency, that is, the fewer the number of members which it returns, the more radical will be the departure from proportionality'.[3] For Hogan this was an *a priori* argument, deduced from the fact that in a large constituency the quota under STV is relatively low, and it is therefore easier for a small party to secure election than in a small constituency, where the quota is relatively high. In his book of 1967 Rae tested this proposition empirically in his cross-national survey and concluded: 'Electoral formulae designed to produce proportionality depend in large measure upon district magnitudes for their efficacy ... The biases of electoral systems generally tend to advantage large parties over small ones ... These biases are inversely related to proportionality: the greater the proportionality, the weaker the biases, and *vice versa*'.[4]

This proposition may also be tested against the results of the eighteen general elections in our survey. For this purpose we may divide the elections into periods corresponding to the regular revisions of the constituencies; except that the revisions of 1947 and 1961 and those of 1969 and

---

This graph shows the rate of 'terminal' transfers between Fine Gael and Labour from 1961 to 1977, i.e. the votes which were transferred when the last Fine Gael/Labour candidate was elected or eliminated, and the other party *and* Fianna Fáil were still in the count. The percentage of terminal transfers has been calculated for each constituency concerned, and then averaged over the whole country. The numbers of constituencies involved were: Fine Gael to Labour – 4, 7, 9, 7, 9, and Labour to Fine Gael – 13, 11, 18, 13, 13 respectively. Where very few constituencies are involved, the figures must be treated with caution.

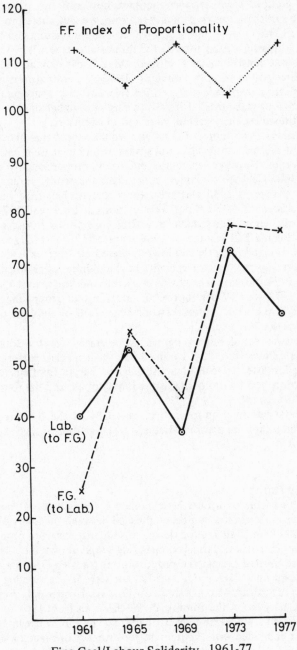

120 ┬
     │ F.F. Index of Proportionality
110 ┤
100 ┤
 90 ┤
 80 ┤
 70 ┤
 60 ┤
 50 ┤
 40 ┤ Lab.
     │ (to F.G.)
 30 ┤
     │ F.G.
 20 ┤ (to Lab.)
 10 ┤
     └──┬──────┬──────┬──────┬──────┬──
      1961   1965   1969   1973   1977

Fine Gael/Labour Solidarity, 1961-77

109

1974 are grouped together, since there was no significant change in constituency size in the latter revision in each case. We will, therefore, have four periods: 1923-35 (some nine-seat, eight-seat and seven-seat constituencies, and only a quarter of the total in the three-seat category); 1935-47 (nine- and eight-seat constituencies abolished, three 7-seat remain, and the number of three-seaters almost doubled); 1947-69 (seven-seaters abolished, henceforth no constituency larger than five-seat, and a varying number of three- and four-seat areas); 1969-77 (a varying number of five- and four-seat constituencies, three-seaters increased to twenty-six).

With these distributions of seats one would expect that in each successive period the bias of the electoral system would increase in favour of the largest parties. However, when the indices of proportionality of Fianna Fáil and Fine Gael are examined in this light the results are inconclusive. The first change in 1935 certainly seems to have benefited Fianna Fáil, but the revision of 1947 did not. The revisions of 1969 (and 1974) did not operate long enough to enable any firm conclusions to be drawn. Admittedly, Fianna Fáil secured in 1969 its second highest index figure; but in 1973 it dropped to its second lowest, while Fine Gael reached its peak. It is also worth noting that the increase in the number of five-seat constituencies in 1974 did not (as might be expected) militate against Fianna Fáil, which in 1977 won 57 per cent of the seats in that group—the same percentage as in the whole country, while Fine Gael, for only the third time, went below the line.

If the vote-seat deviation figures are averaged for the four periods, they are as follows: 1.7, 2.34, 1.6 and 2.32. Again, no clear pattern emerges: the distortion after 1935 is obviously higher than in the first period, but the distortion in the third period is the lowest of all, and the fourth is very close to the second!

The variations in proportionality, especially in the most recent elections, cannot then be attributed solely to constituency size or 'electoral engineering'.

(c) Transfer Patterns

Another variable that must be examined is the pattern of transfers, to see whether a correlation can be established between the index of proportionality of Fianna Fáil and the degree of solidarity between supporters of the two other parties. The accompanying graph shows the Fianna Fáil index figure plotted against the proportion of transfers from Fine Gael to Labour, when only Fianna Fáil and Labour were in the running, and the proportion of transfers from Labour to Fine Gael when only Fianna Fáil and Fine Gael were in the running in the elections from 1961 to 1977 inclusive.[5] Plainly, the highest level of mutual support between Fine Gael and Labour coincided with the poorest performance of Fianna Fáil (1973); while in 1977 Labour voters' support for Fine Gael candidates significantly declined, although Fine Gael support for Labour candidates remained stable—and more Labour transfers went to Fianna Fáil than in 1973.

It would seem, therefore, that the pattern of transfers is the key variable at least in the Irish context. This would mean that the electorate is becoming more volatile than the parties would have believed.

To conclude, then, Irish PR has produced no consistent trend, especially in the last sixteen years, except the over-representation of the largest party.

Conclusion

In surveying the operation of PR in Ireland from the standpoint of 1977, as against 1959, one is immediately struck by the considerable increase in public knowledge of electoral phenomena. It is worth remembering that psephology, the scientific study of elections, is one of the newest branches of political science. The word itself was coined in 1951 by the late R. B. McCallum, author of the first Nuffield College election study, *The British General Election of 1945* (Oxford 1947), and it first appeared in print in 1952.[1] Apart from the publications of the Proportional Representation Society, there was no general survey of the operation of electoral systems available until the second world war. Ferdinand A. Hermens' *Democracy or Anarchy*? (Notre Dame 1940) was the first such study in English and the late James Hogan's *Election and Representation* (Cork 1945) the first to cover Irish elections. The first systematic study of political parties generally was Maurice Duverger's *Political Parties* (London 1954); the first to deal with British parties, R. T. McKenzie's *British Political Parties* (London 1954).

Over the past twenty years, however, a veritable flood of literature has appeared in many languages on all aspects of elections. Possibly the most valuable have been the abstract models of voting behaviour and its impact on party systems, worked out by writers such as Duncan Black, Colin Leys, John Loosemore, V. J. Hanby and the late Robin Farquharson;[2] the inductive works of writers such as Douglas Rae using comparative electoral statistics rigorously to test the validity of accepted generalisations about electoral systems; and the enormous output of works on electoral sociology, beginning in the United States in 1940 and extending to Great Britain a quarter of a century later,[3] in which fresh insights into the complex motivations behind voting are provided through extensive use of survey data. Lastly, there have been many monographs and learned articles on Irish elections and parties, most of which are cited in the text and notes of this book.[4]

The result of all this intellectual activity has been seriously to question previously accepted propositions. For instance, the PR → multiplication of parties → government instability syndrome is no longer regarded as necessary: on the contrary, the connection between parties and electoral systems is now generally conceived as a highly complex relationship of interdependence. When this is accepted, the old PR versus majority system argument loses much of its relevance, since students of elections are much less willing to make categorical assertions about the consequences of one system or the other.

In Ireland too, experience has helped to modify dogmatism. In 1959 it was possible to assert that Irish electoral history had not up to that time held out much hope for the emergence of a pattern of stable one-party government. (Out of thirteen general elections since the establishment of the Irish Free State, only four had produced a single-party majority, while four had produced a stalemate, leading within a year in each case to a fresh election, and two had produced relatively short-lived coalitions.) It seemed reasonable then to assume that the next election would produce another multi-party coalition.

However this prediction was not fulfilled. The first election after 1959 ushered in the era of two-and-a-half parties, and enabled Fianna Fáil to continue in office without having to call a sudden election to 'renew its mandate'. The next four general elections all produced governments with stable majorities. The stability which, in spite of the persistent Northern troubles, is now a fact of Irish political life is more likely to have resulted from the character of the existing parties than from the electoral system. Unlike the small parties of earlier years—and also Labour before 1948— Fianna Fáil, Fine Gael and Labour are all 'majority-bent' parties, and this acts as a constraint upon irresponsible parliamentary behaviour. Even before the coalition arrangement of 1973 it was unlikely that Labour would not have helped to find a way out of a parliamentary deadlock. Moreover, like the West German Free Democrats, Labour has become flexible in its approach to the two big parties, and a future electoral alliance[5] with Fianna Fáil is by no means out of the question. The occupational breakdown of the parties helps to promote this flexibility.

While the PR system in the Irish Republic (unique in sovereign states apart from the small republic of Malta) has over the fifty-seven years of its existence had its ups and downs, it is safe to assert that at present it enjoys widespread public acceptance. Thirty-three years ago, James Hogan wrote that the Irish system was a compromise between PR and the plurality method of voting, with PR still the dominant element in the combination.[6] That judgment is still valid, and the compromise seems likely to endure.

Notes

CHAPTER 1 (pp. 1-4)

1. W. Ullmann, *Law and Politics in the Middle Ages*, London 1975, 155-6.
2. Sir Goronwy Edwards, 'The Emergence of Majority Rule in English Parliamentary Elections', *Transactions of the Royal Historical Society*, 5th series, 14 (1964), 183. This entire article (pp. 175-96) provides a most illuminating discussion of a much forgotten electoral topic.
3. T. Hare, *A Treatise on the Election of Representatives, Parliamentary and Municipal*, London 1859. A Danish politician, Carl Andrae, independently devised an almost identical electoral method in 1855. The first national elections ever under this system occurred in Denmark in 1856 for a limited number of seats in the then unicameral legislature. In 1866 under a new Constitution the Andrae method was restricted to elections for the Upper House. From 1915 both houses were elected by a list form of PR.
4. See E. Lakeman, *How Democracies Vote*, London 1970, 269.
5. H. R. Droop, *Papers of the Juridical Society* III. pt XII (1869), 469.
6. Richard Crossman ed., *The English Constitution*, London 1966, 141.
7. These criteria are borrowed from the best text-book in English on electoral systems, W. J. M. MacKenzie, *Free Elections*, London, 1958.
8. Courtney (a brother-in-law of Beatrice Webb) survived until 1918.
9. Mill, not less than deTocqueville, feared lest universal suffrage might lead to majority tyranny. See J. Hogan, *Election and Representation*, Cork 1945, Chapter 9.
10. The d'Hondt rule (the largest average rule) is the one most generally used in Europe for calculating the electoral quota. See MacKenzie, *op. cit.*, p. 78-9.
11. See P. W. Campbell's contribution in S. E. Finer ed., *Adversary Politics and Electoral Reform*, London, 1975, 143-51.
12. For the second ballot in the Third French Republic see P. M. Williams, *Crisis and Compromise: Politics in the Fourth Republic*, London 1964, 307-9.
13. The method in use in by-elections in Ireland since 1922 is also, of course, an application of the alternative vote.
14. See L. F. Crisp, *Australian National Government*, London 1965, Chapter 5, for an assessment of the Australian experience.

15. During the 1929-31 parliament the minority Labour government of Ramsay MacDonald introduced a bill applying the alternative vote to British parliamentary elections, apparently as the price for Liberal support. The bill passed through the Commons in 1931, but was defeated in the Lords. Since the end of the second world war very few private members' bills have been introduced prescribing a change in the electoral system. See D. E. Butler, *The Electoral System in Britain since 1918*, 2nd ed. Oxford 1963, 58-83, 209.
16. For the assembly election 1973, see R. J. Lawrence, S. Elliott and M. J. Laver, *The Northern Ireland General Election of 1973*, HMSO Cmnd. 5351. For the 1975 election, see Ian MacAllister, *The 1975 Northern Ireland Convention Election*, occasional paper no. 14, Survey Research Centre, Strathclyde University, Glasgow 1975.

CHAPTER 2 (pp. 5-6)
1. See M. Steed, 'The Evolution of the British Electoral System' in S. E. Finer ed., *Adversary Politics and Electoral Reform*, 42-51.
2. Humphreys gave up a career in the civil service to promote the cause of PR. His book, *Proportional Representation*, London 1911, was the first such work in English.
3. See D. E. Butler, *The Electoral System in Britain since 1918*, 6-7.
4. Butler, *op. cit.*, 7-13.
5. For an articulate exposition of their case by a leading Ulster Unionist, see R. MacNeill, *Ulster's Stand for Union*, London 1922.
6. *Freeman's Journal*, 14 Jan. 1911.
7. *Proportional Representation in Ireland*, Dublin and London 1913. Meredith thought that too much propaganda was being made for STV. He favoured a List system (as in Belgium).
8. *Sinn Féin*, 25 Feb. 1911. See also 29 June 1912.
9. See *Representation*, June 1914. This journal (the organ of the PR Society) carries many references to Ireland from this date.
10. *Senate Debates*, vol. 50, 432.

CHAPTER 3 (pp. 7-11)
1. Private bills are rarely debated. There is no other case of a change in the electoral system being made by this procedure in the British parliament.
2. B. Farrell, *The Founding of Dáil Eireann*, Dublin 1971, 46-7.
3. See F. S. L. Lyons, *Ireland since the Famine*, London 1971, 380-97.
4. The strongest presentation of this case is to be found in A. Phillips, *The Revolution in Ireland 1916-1923*, London 1923, 152-3. Phillips, a southern Unionist, was professor of modern history at Trinity College, Dublin.
5. Lyons, *op. cit.*, 397.
5a.P. Mair, 'Labour and the Irish Party System Revisited: Party Competition in the 1920s', *Economic and Social Review*, Vol. 8 (1977), 59-70.
6. See *Representation*, March 1919.
7. See Farrell, *The Founding of Dáil Eireann*, 51-79.
8. *Parliamentary Debates*, 5th series, vol. 114, 175-6.

9. See I. Budge and C. O'Leary, *Belfast: Approach to Crisis*, London 1973, 136-40.
10. For the details of the act see R. J Lawrence, *The Government of Northern Ireland*, Oxford 1965, 15-22.
11. The fullest account of this and all subsequent Stormont elections is in S. Elliott, *The Electoral System in Northern Ireland since 1920*, unpublished PhD thesis, The Queen's University of Belfast 1971.
12. *Freeman's Journal*, 9 May 1921.
13. At the first session of the 'Parliament of Southern Ireland' (June 1921) only the four TCD representatives turned up; at the second only two. So the parliament never formally met until after the Treaty. See note 16.
14. K. Middlemans ed., Tom Jones, *Whitehall Diary*, vol. III, London 1971, provides the best inside story of the negotiations from the British point of view. F. Pakenham (now Earl of Longford), *Peace by Ordeal*, London 1935, is still the most complete account.
15. The *Treaty Debates* are published separately from the *Dáil Debates*.
16. Under Articles 16 and 17 of the Treaty the parliament of Southern Ireland was resurrected and the Provisional Government was made responsible to it. Its sessions were constituted by the sixty pro-Treaty and four Trinity College deputies. See T. D. Williams ed., *The Irish Struggle 1916-1926*, London 1966, especially chapter 10.
17. J. Hogan, *Election and Representation*, Cork 1945, 83.
18. Hogan, *op. cit.*, 87-8.

CHAPTER 4 (pp. 12-16)

1. Dan Breen appears on both panels, but his 3,148 votes are more properly regarded as anti-Treaty. He sat as a Fianna Fáil deputy for Tipperary from 1927 until his retirement in 1965. D. O'Sullivan writes of 'appalling intimidation' by the anti-Treatyites. *The Irish Free State and its Senate*, London 1940, 62.
2. The official name of the anti-Treatyite deputies between the split and the re-emergence of Sinn Féin was Cumann na Poblachta (the Republican Association). See T. P. O'Neill, 'In Search of a Political Path: Irish Republicanism, 1922 to 1927' in G. A. Hayes-McCoy ed., *Historical Studies X*, Galway 1976, 147-8.
3. A striking proof of this bitterness is provided by the fact that de Valera and Cosgrave never met socially from 1922 until shortly before Cosgrave's death in 1965. See the Earl of Longford and T. P. O'Neill, *Eamon de Valera*, Dublin 1970, 456.
4. See *Dáil Debates*, vol. I, 14-29.
5. One of the minority drafts was kindly shown to the present writer by the late Monsignor Alfred O'Rahilly (formerly professor and president of University College, Cork) who was responsible for it. Dr O'Rahilly was opposed to the British-style party system and wished to link deputies more closely with their constituents.
6. L. Kohn, *The Constitution of the Irish Free State*, London 1933, provides the fullest exposition of the provisions of the Constitution.
7. This device, which cut across the principle of Cabinet responsibility,

never really worked and was discontinued after 1927. See B. Chubb, *The Government and Politics of Ireland*, London 1971, 181.

8. This period was extended to twelve years, by the Constitution of 1937, Article 16.

9. In his preface to Kohn, *op. cit.* xi.

10. See above, n. 5.

11. *Select Constitutions of the World*, Dublin 1922. See also A. Headlam-Morley, *The New Democratic Constitutions of Europe*, London 1929.

12. See *Representation*, Mar. 1919, Oct. 1919, Aug. 1922.

13. *Dáil Debates*, vol. I, 355.

14. T. Jones, *Whitehall Diary*, III, 157.

15. *Irish Times*, 19 Jan. 1920.

16. Since the Ulster Unionists had from the beginning been opposed to STV it is not surprising that they abolished it and reverted to the first-past-the-post system soon after they were constitutionally empowered to do so. See N. Mansergh, *The Government of Northern Ireland*, London 1936, 127-36.

17. See *Dáil Debates*, vol. I, 1106-38.

18. The initiative allowed a petition signed by not less than 75,000 voters to force the government to submit an issue (either a law or a constitutional amendment) to a referendum. This was tried by Fianna Fáil with a petition signed by 96,000 voters demanding the abolition of the parliamentary oath (May 1928). The referendum could be used not only for constitutional but ordinary legislation. Both provisions were abolished by the Constitutional Amendment (No. 10) Act, 1928.

19. See T. Lloyd Humberstone, *University Representation*, London 1951.

CHAPTER 5 (pp. 17-45)

1. pp. 96-99.

2. See D. Macardle, *The Irish Republic*, London 1937, 895-900, for a (pro-Sinn Féin) account of harassment during this campaign.

3. M. Manning, *Irish Political Parties*, Dublin 1972, 9-10. This work, though brief, is an essential *vade mecum* for students of Irish parties.

4. *Freeman's Journal*, 28 Apr. 1923.

5. W. Moss, *Political Parties in the Irish Free State*, New York 1933, 29. (This was the only scholarly work on Irish parties to appear until after the second world war.) The protectionist minister for Posts and Telegraphs, J. J. Walsh, unexpectedly retired completely from politics after the second dissolution in 1927.

6. The most recent account of this episode, based on the de Valera archives, is found in T. P. O'Neill, 'In Search of a Political Path: Irish Republicanism, 1922 to 1927', in G. A. Hayes-McCoy ed., *Historical Studies X*, Galway 1976, 147-71. See also P. Pyne, 'The Third Sinn Féin Party, 1923-1926', *Economic and Social Review* I (1970), 29-50, 229-57.

7. J. L. McCracken, *Representative Government in Ireland. A Study of Dáil Eireann, 1919-48*, London 1958, 114.

8. For the early years of the Irish Labour party see A. Mitchell, *Labour in Irish Politics, 1890-1930*, Dublin 1974.

9. Mitchell, *op. cit.*, 75.

10. See Brian Farrell, 'Labour and the Irish Political Party System: a suggested approach to analysis', *Economic and Social Review*, Vol. I (1970), 477-502.

11. For the early history of the NILP, see J. F. Harbinson, *A History of the Northern Ireland Labour Party 1891-1949*, unpublished M.Sc. (Econ.) thesis, The Queen's University of Belfast, 1966.

12. Manning, *op. cit.*, 67.

13. Quoted in Farrell, *loc. cit.*, 502.

14. Mitchell, *op. cit.*, 130.

15. Manning, *op. cit.*, 68-9.

16. A. Mitchell, 'William O'Brien, 1881-1968, and the Irish Labour Movement', *Studies* LX (1971), 311-31. See also E. Larkin, *James Larkin: Irish Labour Leader 1876-1947*, London 1965, 261-74.

17. Manning, *op. cit.*, 93-6; Moss, *op. cit.*, 39-40, 57-9.

18. See R. Fanning, 'Leadership and transition from the politics of revolution to the politics of party: the example of Ireland 1914-1939', a paper given at the *Fourteenth International Congress of Historical Sciences*, San Francisco 1975.

19. Four members of the Second Dáil were professors or lecturers in the National University of Ireland.

20. T. D. Williams ed., *The Irish Struggle 1916-1926*, London 1966, 67-77, 117-28, 183-93.

21. See J. Bowyer Bell, *The Secret Army: A History of the IRA 1916-1970*, London 1970, for a discussion of the extreme Republican ideology.

22. Moss, *Political Parties in the Irish Free State*, 54-108.

23. Of the electorate in 1923, middle-aged voters could remember Parnell and the very oldest voters (eighty-five and over) could remember O'Connell.

24. See D. E. Butler, *The Electoral System in Britain since 1918*, 2nd ed. Oxford 1963, 43-4, 172-78.

25. One of the ex-Unionists, Major Bryan Cooper, who had sat as a Unionist member at Westminster, was elected as an Independent deputy for Dublin County in 1923. In September 1927, he joined Cumann na nGaedheal, which provoked Fianna Fáil into coining one of the most memorable electioneering slogans of these years, 'Cooper's Dip for Free State Sheep'. (Cooper's Sheep Dip was universally sold in rural Ireland.)

26. O'Neill, *loc. cit.*, 159-71.

27. Pyne, *loc. cit.*, 46.

28. N. Mansergh, *The Irish Free State, Its Government and Politics*, London 1934, 289-90.

29. *Dáil Debates*, vol. 22, 1615-16.

30. Manning, *op. cit.*, 88.

31. O'Sullivan, *The Irish Free State and its Senate*, 183, 190, 193.

32. Moss, *op. cit.*, 141-5; Manning, *op. cit.*, 91-3.

33. There is no scholarly study in print of the various Irish communist

groups from the first Communist Party of Ireland (1921-23) to the second (1933-41). For the references in this chapter I am indebted to M. Milotte, 'Communist Politics in Ireland 1916-1945', unpublished Ph.D. thesis, The Queen's University of Belfast, 1977.

34. Moss devotes three successive chapters to the general elections of June 1927, September 1927 and 1932. Moss, *op. cit.*, 141-88.

35. Professor Michael Hayes, Ceann Comhairle from 1922 until 1932, was a Cumann na nGaedheal deputy for the National University, who had held ministerial office in the Second Dáil. After the abolition of university representation in 1935 he served for many years as Fine Gael leader in the Senate.

36. See Mitchell, *Labour in Irish Politics*, 270-8.

37. *Irish Independent*, 4 June 1927.

38. *The Leader*, Christmas 1958.

39. See K. B. Nowlan, 'President Cosgrave's Last Administration' in F. MacManus ed., *The Years of the Great Test, 1926-1939*, Cork 1967, 7-18.

40. Moss, *op. cit.*, 54-108, provides an excellent description of party organisation in the 1920s and early 1930s.

41. Although the Irish Parliamentary Party had often raised election funds in the US, and Sinn Féin did so in 1923, this is the last such case in our period.

42. Ten constitutional amendments were effected between 1922 and 1930. See above, Chap. 4, n. 18.

43. Manning, *op. cit.*, 14.

44. Frank MacDermot, a member of an old Roscommon landowning family, had served in the British Army during the first world war and later spent some years in the United States. He was in his mid-forties when elected to the Dáil as an Independent in 1932. His career in the Centre Party and Fine Gael lasted a mere four years. In 1937 he did not offer himself for reelection, but was appointed as one of the Taoiseach's eleven nominees to the new Senate in 1938. After the war he retired to France, whence he frequently contributed rather querulous letters to the Irish newspapers. He died in 1975. James Dillon, the son of John Dillon, the last leader of the Irish Parliamentary Party, enjoyed a much longer career in politics. Also elected as an Independent in 1932 (aged thirty), he helped to form the Centre Party, which merged with Cumann na nGaedheal in 1933. Dillon was deputy leader to Cosgrave from 1935 to 1942 when he was expelled from Fine Gael for advocating Irish entry into the war. Re-elected as an Independent in 1943, 1944 and 1948, Dillon was Minister for Agriculture in both coalition governments. He rejoined Fine Gael in 1952, succeeded to the leadership in 1959—which he held until 1965, and sat on in the Dáil as an active backbencher until 1969.

45. Moss, *op. cit.*, 192.

46. See above, p. 23.

47. *Irish Times*, 15 June 1938.

48. The standard work on this movement is M. Manning, *The Blueshirts*, Dublin 1971.

49. *Cork Examiner*, 1-3 Sept. 1934.

119

50. Manning, *The Blueshirts*, 198-207.
51. The Earl of Longford and T. P. O'Neill, *Eamon de Valera*, 139-40, 293.
52. See below, p. 102.
53. *Dáil Debates.*, vol. 67, 1341-56.
54. *Ibid.*
55. *Irish Times*, 3 June 1938.
56. *Ibid.*
57. *Irish Times*, 23 June 1938. For the other contributions see *Irish Times*, 4, 6, 10, 15 and 16 June 1938.
58. *Irish Times*, 15 June 1938. See above, 28.
59. The first and second amendments to the Constitution (conferring emergency powers on the government following the outbreak of the second world war) were effected by this provision (1939 and 1941).
60. See *Dáil Debates*, vol. 67, 1343-6, for de Valera's defence of the electoral system. The official biography is silent as to the reason why PR was incorporated into the Constitution.
61. Moss, *op. cit.*, 54 n. 1. Moss also observed that (in 1933) Cosgrave's party 'feel confident that stupid blunders and a revulsion of feeling will deliver their government back to them' (p. 194).
62. For de Valera's skilful handling of the problems of neutrality see J. T. Carroll, *Ireland in the War Years, 1939-45*, Newton Abbot, 1975.
63. J. Hogan, *Election and Representation*, 33.
64. The inaugural meeting in 1938 'attracted delegates from all parts of the west'. (Manning, *Irish Political Parties*, 99.)
65. Under the 1937 Constitution the official name of the Prime Minister is *An Taoiseach*, and the deputy Prime Minister *An Tanaiste*. The name of the state, 'Eire', was dropped officially in 1949 because it was being used as a convenient synonym for the twenty-six counties, especially in Great Britain. The two Cumann na nGaedheal ex-ministers defeated in 1943 were General Richard Mulcahy and Professor J. M. O'Sullivan.
66. See E. Rumpf and A. C. Hepburn, *Nationalism and Socialism in Ireland*, Liverpool 1977, 149-52.
67. The leader was James Everett, who was first elected to the Dáil in 1922.
68. *Irish Independent*, 2 June 1944. Hogan, *Election and Representation*, 31-6, 70-78, writes acutely about the general elections of 1943 and 1944.
69. *News Review*, Dec. 1945 ('Exit Fine Gael').
70. Mr Flanagan was one of the three recruits to the Fine Gael benches in 1952, and served as a parliamentary secretary (1954-7) and Minister for Defence (1976-7).
71. See Bowyer Bell, *The Secret Army*, Chapter 7.
72. Two of the Clann deputies elected in 1948 had been active in subversive organisations in the 1930s.
73. See 'Ireland's Man of Destiny', *Life* magazine, Jan. 1948.
74. Only three new Fine Gael TDs were elected in 1943 and 1944; two of

them, Liam Cosgrave and Maurice Dockrell, were sons of sitting TDs. Only E. J. Coogan (1944) was not a relative of a former deputy.

75. *Irish Independent, Irish Press*, 6 Feb. 1948.
76. One candidate, P. Collins (North Galway), is erroneously entered as 'C na P' in the *Copies of the Public Notices of the Results of the Elections and of the Transfers of Votes* for 1948. His correct designation is 'C na T'. (I owe this correction to Mr Michael Gallagher.)
77. Under the Constitution of 1937 (following the Free State Constitution) the Attorney General is not a member of the government.
78. McGilligan, Minister for Industry and Commerce 1924-32, served as Minister for Finance (1948-51) and Attorney General (1954-7). He was defeated in the general election of 1965.
79. B. Chubb, *The Government and Politics of Ireland*, 169, 182-3.
80. B. Farrell, *Chairman or Chief? The Role of Taoiseach in Irish Government*, Dublin 1971, 42-54.
81. *Dáil Debates*, vol. 110, 25.
82. *Sunday Independent*, 5 Sept. 1948, carried a 'scoop' article headed 'External Relations Act to go'. This apparently forced Costello's hand —see F. S. L. Lyons, 'The Years of Adjustment, 1945-1951' in T. D. Williams and K. B. Nowlan eds., *Ireland in the War Years and After*, Dublin 1969, 71-4.
83. See *Dáil Debates*, vol. 113, 347-423 for Costello's and de Valera's speeches on the second stage of the bill.
84. All three NILP seats were lost in 1949. In 1958 four NILP candidates were elected to the Stormont House of Commons.
85. A mass meeting was held in Dublin addressed by the Taoiseach and all party leaders, including de Valera.
86. See J. H. Whyte, *Church and State in Modern Ireland 1923-1970*, Dublin 1971, chapter 7.
87. See *Irish Times* editorial, 12 Apr. 1951 ('Contra Mundum').
88. The Ulster Unionist Council reprinted the debates on Browne's resignation *(Dáil Debates*, vol. 125, 666-804 and 894-954) verbatim and without comment.
89. B. Inglis, 'Candidates in Eire', *The Spectator*, 25 May 1951.
90. The Electoral (Chairman of Dáil Eireann) Acts 1927 to 1963 allowed the outgoing Ceann Comhairle an automatic return for the constituency of his choice in a general election; the purpose was to spare a sitting Ceann Comhairle the necessity of indulging in partisan electioneering—and to avoid his defeat, if he did not do so. The first Ceann Comhairle, Michael Hayes, was defeated for re-election to the post in a party vote after the 1932 election by Frank Fahy, then a Fianna Fáil front-bencher. In 1951 it was known before the general election that Fahy would not offer himself for re-election to the chair; nevertheless, he availed himself of the unopposed return privilege and after the election retired to the Fianna Fáil benches which he had left nineteen years before. There was some grumbling from the Fine Gael benches, but Fahy, in effect, started a new tradition. His two successors, Patrick Hogan (Lab., 1951-67) and Cormac Breslin (FF, 1967-73), sat on in the Dáil for a 'free term' after their retirement from the

chair. Fahy and Hogan both died during their free terms, and Breslin retired from politics in 1977 after forty years in the Dáil. Sean Treacy (Lab.), elected Ceann Comhairle in 1973, was defeated for re-election to the post on a party vote when the Dáil met after the June 1977 election by Joseph Brennan (FF) and returned to the Labour ranks.

91. The third recruit to Fine Gael was a midland deputy who had left the party in 1947. See above, 39.
92. See *Irish Times*, 12 May 1954.
93. Except for the Blueshirt period. In 1933 Warner Moss presciently noted the need of Cosgrave's party to attract young voters, *Political Parties in the Irish Free State*, 195.
94. See B. Chubb's valuable study, 'Ireland 1957', in D. E. Butler ed., *Elections Abroad*, London 1959, 183-222.
95. See above, 23.
96. To date Browne's political odyssey has been as follows: Clann na Poblachta (1948-51), Independent (1951-2), Fianna Fáil (1952-7), Independent (1957-8), National Progressive Democrat (1958-63), Labour (1963-77), Socialist Labour (1977).

CHAPTER 6 (pp. 46-58)

1. *Sunday Independent*, 5 Sept. 1948. See Chap. 5, n. 82.
2. This policy of non-commitment—a possible by-product of wartime censorship—is very manifest in the *Independent* newspapers in the immediate post-war period. There was no editorial comment on the repeal of the External Relations Act (1948), the decision not to enter NATO (Feb. 1949), the Browne resignation (1951), nor the recrudescence of subversive activities in the North (1955-6). The same was true of the *Irish Press* (excepting the External Relations Act). The leading article in the *Independent* on 12 April 1951 (the day after Browne's resignation) was on the dismissal of General MacArthur!
3. *Irish Times*, 29 Aug. 1958.
4. See above, 31.
5. *Irish Press*, 9 Sept. 1958.
6. *Irish Times, Irish Independent*, 9 Sept. 1958.
7. *Irish Times*, 29-31 Oct. 1958.
8. See *Dáil Debates*, vol. 172, 839-42, for Dillon's argument for the alternative vote as 'a second worst' solution.
9. Addressing a Fine Gael meeting in Dublin, Costello said that what the country needed was reduced taxation, not a new electoral system. *Irish Times*, 2 Oct. 1958.
10. *National Observer*, May 1959.
11. *Dáil Debates*, vol. 171, 7-8.
12. The best contemporary analysis of the debates is to be found in Garret FitzGerald, 'PR—The Great Debate', *Studies* XLVIII (1959), 1-20. The debates in the Dáil cover two volumes (171 and 172) of the official record.
13. By custom all party leaders have the privilege of speaking to the first reading of a bill, if they wish to do so.
14. Here de Valera was clearly consistent. His attitude in 1938 has already been discussed (see above, 30ff.). In subsequent election cam-

paigns his opposition to PR hardened, but he always asserted that the electoral system could not be an issue at a general election, since a special referendum was needed.

15. *Irish Times,* 27 Nov. 1958.
16. The books most frequently cited in these debates were E. Lakeman and J. D. Lambert, *Voting in Democracies,* London 1955, and J. F. S. Ross, *The Irish Election System,* London 1959, both of which are too partial to PR. For the evidence on the other side of the case see F. A. Hermens, *Democracy or Anarchy? A Study of Proportional Representation,* Notre Dame 1941, and Maurice Duverger, *Political Parties,* Eng. trans. London 1954.
17. *Dáil Debates,* vol. 171, 999-1000.
18. *Ibid.,* 1025.
19. *Ibid.,* 1521.
20. This statement was not made in the Dáil, but appeared in the Protestant journal, *Focus,* Feb. 1959, 18. The article was entitled 'Electoral Reform in the Republic'.
21. See above, 24.
22. *Dáil Debates,* vol. 171, 2345-8.
23. *Irish Times,* 6 Dec. 1958.
24. Informed contributions to the discussion were disappointingly few. FitzGerald's article, cited above, was mainly descriptive; Professor Hogan wrote a short article, 'The Electoral Problem' in the *Irish Ecclesiastical Record* (June 1959), and *Trinity News* of Trinity College, Dublin, devoted an entire issue to a symposium on PR, one of the contributions to which (Basil Chubb, 'An Academic View') was afterwards reprinted by the *Irish Times,* 28 April 1959. The *Tuairm* pamphlet, referred to below, was entitled *PR—For or Against,* Dublin 1959.
25. *Irish Times,* 9 Jan. 1959.
26. *Ibid.,* 18 June 1959. In the official biography, the Earl of Longford and T. P. O'Neill, *Eamon de Valera,* it is stated that at a party meeting in 'mid-January' 1959, de Valera announced that 'he had for a considerable time made up his mind that it would not be in the interests either of the country or the Party' that he should lead Fianna Fáil in the next election (p. 446). Longford and O'Neill imply that it was Oscar Traynor who suggested that de Valera stand for the presidency (p. 447). Brian Farrell in *Chairman or Chief?* examines various allegations that some senior colleagues put pressure on de Valera to retire, and concludes: 'On balance, then, it appears that de Valera relinquished office of his own accord' (p. 41).
27. For the debates, see *Dáil Debates,* vol. 172, 16-126, 1071-1121; vol. 173, 126-82, 379-83. The opposition vainly tried to bring back the form of the ballot paper prescribed by the Referendum Act, 1942 (which had never been used), according to which the proposal to be submitted to referendum must be stated on the ballot paper, 'in the same terms as nearly as may be as such proposal is stated in the Bill' (Sec. 5). To the opposition charge that the 1942 Act would give the voters valuable information denied to them by the new bill, Blaney could make no satisfactory reply.

28. A certain heavy-handedness by the Leas Ceann Comhairle inflamed the already sensitive opposition and put all de Valera's prudence to the test. See *Dáil Debates*, vol. 172, 182-207.
29. *Ibid.*, 796.
30. *Ibid.*, 960.
31. *Ibid.*, 1284-96.
32. See *Senate Debates*, vol. 50, 249-888. The second reading debate covers almost the entire volume.
33. The National University senators were Professor George O'Brien (economist), Professor P. M. Quinlan (mathematical physicist) and Dr H. L. Barniville (surgeon). The Trinity College senators were Professor W. B. Stanford (classicist), Professor W. R. Fearon (pathologist) and Dr. Owen Sheehy Skeffington, a French scholar.
34. *Irish Independent*, 20 Mar. 1959.
35. The appeal was published in all the newspapers of 21 March 1959. Professor Quinlan also wrote numerous letters to the provincial press.
36. The form of the ballot paper made the government bill, not the electoral system, the subject of the voter's choice. Thus those who opposed PR had to vote 'yes', those who supported it, 'no'.
37. *Irish Times*, 15 May 1959.
38. 'PR in Ireland', *Irish Times*, 20-25 Apr. 1959.
39. See *PR—For or Against*.
40. Sheldon's broadcast was on 10 June. Characteristically he had opposed the Republic of Ireland Bill of 1948 on the ground that it involved a breach of Fine Gael's election pledges.
41. *Irish Times*, 30 May 1959.
42. *Irish Times*, 12 June 1959. See also *Liberty* (June 1959), the official organ of the Irish Transport and General Workers' Union.
43. *Irish Times*, 6 Dec. 1958.
44. For the official figures see *Iris Ofigiuil*, 23 June 1959.
45. See table in C. O'Leary, *The Irish Republic and its Experiment with Proportional Representation*, Notre Dame, Indiana, 1961, 86.
46. *Irish Review and Annual*, 1 Jan. 1960, 7.

CHAPTER 7 (pp. 59-92)
1. B. Farrell, *Chairman or Chief?* 70-72.
2. Farrell, *op. cit.*, 18.
3. B. Chubb, in D. E. Butler ed., *Elections Abroad*, London 1959, 200.
4. See *Economic Development* (Pr. 4803), 1958, 4.
5. F. S. L. Lyons, *Ireland since the Famine*, London 1971, 615.
6. See B. Inglis, *West Briton*, London 1962, for a journalist's impressions of that period.
7. Farrell, *op. cit.*, 72.
8. See *Dáil Debates*, vol. 177, 377-459, 488-516, 1058-1124; also B. Chubb, *The Government and Politics of Ireland*, London 1971, 149-50, for a brief discussion of this bill. (The second reading was unopposed).
9. For details of the judgment see *Irish Law Reports* 1961, 114-156.
10. *Irish Law Reports* 1961, 182.
11. See article by 'a student of politics', *Sunday Press*, 15 Oct. 1961.

12. See *What Fine Gael Stands For*, Dublin 1961.
13. See interview with Corish, *Sunday Independent*, 15 Oct. 1961, justifying his attitude.
14. *Irish Independent*, 4 Oct. 1961.
15. See M. Manning, *Irish Political Parties*, 99-106, for a balanced assessment of the two Clanns.
16. See analysis of the Second Programme in *Irish Times*, 22 Aug. 1963.
17. Before the application was even tabled Lemass had to make a special tour of the six countries, urging the governments to use their influence to speed up the process. Nevertheless, up to January 1963 negotiations were only at the bureaucratic level, without ministerial involvement.
18. Thornley returned to the same theme in another series in the *Irish Times* (1-3 June 1964) and *Studies* (Spring 1964), in which he claimed that no party could attain an overall majority without winning 550,000 votes, and 'if this is a correct prognosis we can anticipate an era of coalition or minority government' (L111. 17).
19. From then until his enforced resignation in April 1969, O'Neill enjoyed immense popularity in the Republic. In January 1969 readers of the *Sunday Independent* voted him 'Man of the Year'.
20. D. Thornley, 'The Fianna Fáil Party' (one of three articles on the major parties) *Irish Times*, 1 Apr. 1965.
21. It is well to remember that in 1965 the weekly non-contributory old age pension was a mere £1. 17s. 6d!
22. *Irish Times*, 27 May 1964.
23. *Irish Times*, 24-6 Mar. 1965.
24. See editorial in *Irish Independent*, 24 Mar. 1965 ('Has Declan Costello made off with the Labour Party's clothes?').
25. See Chubb, *op cit.*, 134.
26. *Ibid.*
27. The best known commentators were 'Backbencher' (John Healy) in the *Irish Times*, Michael Mills of the *Irish Press* and Arthur Noonan of the *Irish Independent*.
28. See table in Manning, *op. cit.*, 87.
29. *Irish Times*, 15 Apr. 1965.
30. *Ibid.*, 20, 21 Apr. 1965.
31. See Farrell, *op. cit.*, 72-7 for a discussion of this episode. He noted that when Lynch met the Dáil after his election he stated that he 'was not Taoiseach in a caretaker capacity'. (*Ibid.*, 75).
32. Twenty arguments in favour of and twelve against changing the system were presented. The report also gave an exposition of the mechanics of the main proportional and majority systems. *See Report of the Committee on the Constitution*, (Pr. 9817), 1967.
33. See *Irish Times*, 15, 16, 22, 31 Jan; 1 Feb. 1968, for articles by Basil Chubb, David Thornley, John Kelly and the present writer.
34. *Dáil Debates*, vol. 232, 1944-59.
35. Almost the whole of vol. 233, and large sections of vols. 234 and 235 of the *Dáil Debates* are taken up by the debates on the bills. See Chap. 6, n. 12.
36. See *Dáil Debates*, vol. 235, 747-50, 774-822, 854-913, 1311-19. After

four days' debate the amendment was rejected, without a division. (In 1969 Norton joined Fianna Fáil but failed to secure re-election for his Kildare constituency.)

37. Early in the campaign, the *Sunday Independent* held a postal ballot of its readers which resulted in 91 per cent of the respondents expressing opposition to the change (3 Mar. 1968).
38. See F. A. Hermens in *Irish Times*, 25 Sept. 1968, and C. O'Leary, *Irish Press*, 1 Oct. 1968. A random sample of the letter columns in the *Times* or *Independent* at any time between January and October 1968 will produce a preponderance of letters in support of the status quo.
39. See D. Thornley, 'Television and Politics', *Administration* 15 (1967), 217-25.
40. *Dáil Debates*, vol. 232, 1988-92.
41. See E. Lakeman, 'The Irish Voter—1968 Pattern', *Parliamentary Affairs*, 22 (1968-9), 170-74.
42. For the second stage debate, see *Dáil Debates* vol. 237, 1219-94, 1339-65, 1389-1440, 1800-1842, 1935-2039, 2628-54.
43. *Ibid.* 1128-42.
44. M. Gallagher, 'Disproportionality in a Proportional Representation System: The Irish Experience', *Political Studies* XXIII (Dec. 1975), 512. The whole article (pp. 501-13) is an excellent short discussion of the modes in which the Irish system deviates from proportionality.
45. *Dáil Debates*, vol. 237, 1817.
46. *Ibid.*, 1219-29, 2628-54. (In his closing speech Boland complained that the opposition had not left him sufficient parliamentary time to reply to their allegations.)
47. For a penetrating analysis of the role of the Labour Party in the 1969 election, see M. A. Busteed and H. Mason, 'Irish Labour in the 1969 Election', *Political Studies* XVIII (Sept. 1970), 373-9.
48. See *The New Republic. The Official Programme of the Labour Party*, Dublin 1969, and *Election News*, June 1969.
49. Between 1969 and his return to the Dáil in 1973, Costello devoted himself to his legal practice.
50. For campaign details see especially *Irish Times*, 30 May, 4, 5, 6, 11, 14 June 1969.
51. A remarkable example of the falling off of rural support was the fate of Rickard Deasy, a large farmer in Tipperary, who had secured national fame by leading a march of *Macra na Feirme* (the National Farmers' Association), of which he was president, to Dublin in 1967 in protest against government agricultural policies. In 1969 he stood as a Labour candidate in North Tipperary—where the party frequently won a seat—but came bottom of the poll with 517 votes.
52. See J. Knight and N. Baxter-Moore, *Republic of Ireland: The General Elections of 1969 and 1973*, London, 1973, 14. This is the first study to reproduce the details of the counts in all the constituencies in an Irish general election. See also Ted Nealon, *Ireland: A Parliamentary Directory 1973-74*, Dublin 1974.
53. *Irish Times*, 21 June 1969.
54. See especially M. Hastings, *Ulster 1969*, London 1970.

55. The best works on the IRA are J. Bowyer Bell, *The Secret Army* and T. P. Coogan, *The IRA*, London 1970.
56. See above, 22.
57. One (Sean Sherwin) joined Aontacht Eireann (its only sitting deputy); the other was expelled from the party for voting against a fiscal measure, but was reinstated before the election of 1973. AE lasted until 1976.
58. See C. Glennon's appreciation of Brendan Corish, *Irish Independent*, 27 June 1977.
59. A succinct account of the campaign is given by Nicolas Baxter-Moore in *The General Elections of 1969 and 1973*, 17-21.
60. He was later elected to the Senate for the Dublin University constituency, as an Independent.
61. *Limerick Leader*, 23 Feb. 1969.
62. See below, 91.
63. This was the first occasion that an outgoing Minister failed to retain his seat, since the defeat of Peter Hughes, Minister for Defence, in June 1927.
64. See above, p. 73; also Knight and Baxter-Moore *op. cit.*, 23-7, 31-5.
65. In the presidential election of 1945 the Fine Gael candidate, General Sean MacEoin, secured 30.9 per cent of the first preferences; in the 1948 general election Fine Gael secured only 19.8 per cent of the national vote.
66. See *Irish Press*, 4 Sept. 1976; *Hibernia*, Sept. 1976.
67. For a discussion of the significance of these figures see *Irish Times*, 3 June 1977.
68. See *Irish Times*, especially 25 Oct., 1 Nov. 1976.
69. See article by Richard Sinnott and Brendan Whelan, 'Fianna Fáil's return was carefully planned', *Irish Times*, 30 June 1977.
70. *Dáil Debates*, vol. 265, 95 (28 Mar. 1973).
71. M. Gallagher, *loc. cit.*, 512.
72. *Dáil Debates*, vol. 268, 1983-87.
73. For Molloy's speech, see *Dáil Debates*, vol. 268, 1987-2019.
74. *Ibid.*, 2030.
75. For the debate, see *Ibid.*, vol. 268, 1987-2059; vol. 269, 311-74, 600-92, 1024-1132, 1383-1490.
76. *Evening Echo*, 29 Oct. 1973.
77. See *Dáil Debates*, vol. 269, 1464-89.
78. *Ibid.*, 1488.
79. P. Mair and M. Laver, 'Proportionality, PR and STV in Ireland', *Political Studies* XXIII (Dec. 1975), 496.
80. See P. M. Sacks' recent study, *The Donegal Mafia*, London and New Haven 1976.
81. See *Irish Times* and *Irish Press*, 23 May 1977.
82. *Irish Press*, 26 May 1977.
83. *Hibernia*, 27 May 1977.
84. *Irish Times*, 1 June 1977.
85. *Hibernia*, 10 June 1977.

86. For an academic analysis of the unemployment problem see R. Keatinge, *Irish Times*, 3 June 1977; also R. C. Geary and M. Dempsey, *A study of Schemes for the Relief of Unemployment in Ireland*, Economic & Social Research Institute, Dublin 1977, which projected an unemployment rate of 16.5 per cent by 1980, unless existing policies were changed.
87. See *Irish Times* editorial, 10 June 1977.
88. *Irish Independent*, 11 June 1977.
89. The polls were published in full in the *Irish Times*, 3, 10, and 14 June 1977.
90. Michael Finlan. See his highly amusing apologia in the *Irish Times*, 27 June 1977.
91. On the formation of the Coalition Declan Costello had been appointed Attorney General, a non-Cabinet post. Shortly before the 1977 election he was appointed to a High Court judgeship.
92. Sinnott and Whelan *(loc. cit.)* in analysing pre-election polls concluded that the proportion of under twenty-fives voting Fianna Fáil was only slightly above their proportion in the electorate.

CHAPTER 8 (pp. 93-99)
1. W. Moss, *Political Parties in the Irish Free State*, 136.
2. J. L. McCracken, *Representative Government in Ireland: A Study of Dáil Eireann, 1919-48*, 114-7.
3. The first survey-based study of political socialisation (or acculturation) in Ireland—a survey of school children, aged eleven to eighteen, conducted in June 1972—showed that parental influence, while still the most important, is not the sole determinant of partisan political attitudes. See J. Raven & C. T. Whelan, P. A. Pfretzschner and D. M. Borock, *Political Culture in Ireland: The Views of Two Generations*, Dublin 1976, 85-199.
4. M. Duverger, *Les Partis Politiques*, translated into English as *Political Parties*, 1954.
5. L. Epstein, *Political Parties in Western Democracies*, New York 1967; J. La Palombara and M. Weiner eds., *Political Parties and Political Development*, Princeton 1966; S. Henig and J. Pinder eds., *European Political Parties*, London 1969.
6. S. M. Lipset and S. Rokkan, *Party Systems and Voter Alignments: Cross-National Perspectives*, New York 1967, 1-64.
7. The first scholar to adopt this approach was Ernest Rumpf whose *Nationalismus und Sozialismus in Irland* (1959) was not translated into English until 1977; cf. E. Rumpf and A. C. Hepburn, *Nationalism and Socialism in Twentieth-century Ireland*, especially Chapters 2 and 3. For Tom Garvin's views, see 'Political Cleavages, Party Politics and Urbanisation in Ireland: the Case of the Periphery-Dominated Centre', *European Journal of Political Research*, vol. 2 (1974), 307-27; 'Nationalist Elites, Irish Voters and Irish Political Development: a Comparative Perspective', *Economic and Social Review*, vol. 8 (July 1977), 161-86, and 'Local Party Activists in Dublin:

Socialisation, Recruitment and Incentives', *British Journal of Political Science,* vol. 6 (July 1976), 369-80. The first article listed above was criticised by R. K. Carty, 'Social Cleavages and Party Systems: a Reconsideration of the Irish Case', *European Journal of Political Research* (1976), to which Garvin wrote a spirited reply, 'Comment on Dr. Carty's Rejoinder', *Ibid,* vol. 4 (1976), 195-203, 204.

8. B. Chubb, 'Going about Persecuting Civil Servants: the Role of the Irish Parliamentary Representative', *Political Studies,* XI (Oct. 1963), 272-86. M. Bax, *Harpstrings and Confessions: Machine-Style Politics in the Irish Republic,* Assen 1976, (a study of an unnamed constituency, presumably in Cork), and P. Sacks, *The Donegal Mafia.*

9. J. Blondel, *An Introduction to Comparative Government,* London 1969, 158. The whole of Chapter 8 (pp. 153-76) is relevant here.

10. G. Sartori, *Parties and Party Systems. A framework for analysis,* I, Cambridge 1976.

CHAPTER 9 (pp. 100-111)

1. C. O'Leary, *The Irish Republic and Its Experiment with Proportional Representation,* 50-52.

2. See D. W. Rae, *The Political Consequences of Electoral Laws,* revised ed. New Haven and London 1971, 84 *et seq.* Rae's formula is

$$I = \sum_{i=1}^{N} \frac{|T_i - S_i|}{N}$$

where T is a party's share of the votes, S its share of the seats, N the number of competing parties and I the average vote-seat deviation. These deviations are summed in absolute numbers, so that minus and plus differences are counted positively together.

3. J. Hogan, *Election and Representation,* 13.

4. Rae, *op. cit.,* 119-20.

5. See A. S. Cohan, R. D. McKinlay and A. Mughan, 'The Used Vote and Electoral Outcomes: the Irish General Election of 1973', *British Journal of Political Science,* vol. 5 (1975), 363-83.

CONCLUSION (pp. 112-113)

1. D. E. Butler, *The British General Election of 1951,* London 1952, 1.

2. D. Black, *The Theory of Committees and Elections,* Cambridge 1958; C. Leys, 'Models, Theories and the Theory of Political Parties' in H. Eckstein and D. Apter, *Comparative Politics,* New York 1963, 305-15; and J. Loosemore and V. J. Hanby, 'The Theoretical Limits of Maximum Distortion: Some Analytic Expressions for Electoral Systems', *British Journal of Political Science,* vol. I. (1971), 467-77.

3. A Campbell, P. Converse, W. Miller and D. Stokes, *The American Voter,* Michigan 1941; D. E. Butler and D. Stokes, *Political Change in Britain,* London 1967.

4. Among those omitted for reasons of space is the interesting research

of Brendan Walsh and Christopher Robson into the potentialities of alphabetical voting. In two studies, *Alphabetical Voting: A Study of the 1973 General Election,* Economic and Social Research Institute, Dublin 1973, and in the *Irish Times,* 30 June 1977, these scholars establish that in the first election 55 per cent of candidates elected had names with first letter A-G, compared with 38 per cent of the whole population, while in the latter election the figure was 50 per cent. Walsh and Robson conclude that a significant number of voters vote right down the party ticket, and suggest as a reform that the ordering of names on ballot papers should be determined by lot.

5. This is hinted at in an interview with Michael O'Leary, the outgoing Minister for Labour, *Sunday Independent,* 26 June 1977.

6. Hogan, *op. cit.,* 15.

Index

d'Hondt, Victor, 3, 114
Dillon, James, 27-8, 34, 36, 43, 51-65 passim, 74, 119; on alternative vote, 54, 68, 122
Dillon, John, 9
Dockrell, Maurice, 121
Donegan, P.S., 83
Donnellan, Michael, 35, 63
Droop quota, 2, 114
Duverger, Maurice, 96, 99, 112

Elections, 1918, 7-8, 1920 (local), 8-9, 14; 1921, 9, 17; 1922 (Pact), 10-13, 19; 1923, 17-21; 1927 (June), 23-5, 52, 127; 1927 (Sept.), 23-6; 1932, 26; 1933, 27-8; 1937, 29-30, 33; 1938, 30-3; 1943, 35-7; 1944, 37-8; 1948, 38-40; 1951, 42-3; 1954, 43-4; 1957, 44-5; 1961, 62-3; 1965, 64-6; 1969, 72-4; 1973, 77-81; 1977, 86-92
Electoral Acts, 1923, 15-6; 1963, 79; constituency revisions, 1935, 29; 1947, 38-9; 1959, 61; 1961, 61-2; 1969, 70-2; 1974, 83-6
Emergency Powers Act 1976, 82-3
Everett, James, 19, 39, 120

Fahy, Frank, 43, 121-2
Farmers' Party, 19-20, 24, 27, 31, 100
Fianna Fail
  origin, 22
  organisation, 25
  in power, 26
  end of first government, 40
  attitude to P.R., 47-8
Fine Gael
  origin, 28
  and neutrality, 35
  decline, 36-9
  recovery, 44
  attitude to P.R., 48-9, 68
FitzGerald, Desmond, 34
FitzGerald, Garret, 64-6, 71, 73, 79, 81-4, 90, 92, 122
Fitzpatrick, T.J., 70, 85
Flanagan, O.J., 38, 43, 120

Gallagher, Michael, 71, 121, 126
Gallup Polls, Ltd., 83, 93
Garvin, Tom, 97, 128-9
Griffith, Arthur, 6-10, 13-15

Halligan, Brendan, 86, 91

Hare System. See Single Transferable Vote.
Hare, Thomas, 1-2, 114
Haughey, Charles, 59, 66-7, 73-6, 78, 87, 92
Hayes, Prof. Michael, 119, 121
Hermens, Prof. F.A., 69, 112, 126
Hillery, Dr P.J., 59, 82-3
Hogan, Prof. James, 28, 32-3, 108, 112-3
Hogan, Patrick (C. na G.), 33-4
Hogan, Patrick (Lab.), 121-2
Hughes, Peter, 127
Humphreys, J.H., 5, 8, 32, 52, 115

Irish Congress of Trade Unions, 57
Irish Marketing Surveys Ltd., 83, 89, 93
Irish Republican Army, original, 9-10; after 1922, 20, 27-8, 32, 35, 38, 41, 44; Official, 75; Provisional, 20, 75-6, 81
Irish Transport and General Workers' Union, 18-19, 36, 72
Irish Worker League, 23-4, 105

Johnson, Thomas, 19, 24

Keating, Justin, 72, 78, 91
Kelly, Prof. John, 73, 84-5, 87, 125
Kennedy, Chief Justice Hugh, 14

Labour Party
  origin, 18-19
  supports Fianna Fail, 26
  split, 36-7
  first and second coalitions, 40, 43-4
  independent policy, 60
  third coalition, 81
Lakeman, Enid, 52, 69
Larkin, James (Jr.), 24, 36, 39
Larkin, James (Sr.), 18-19, 23-4, 36-7, 39, 105
Lemass, Noel, 86
Lemass, Sean, 22, 49, 59-67, 74, 125
Lenihan, Brian, 80
Liaison Committee of the Left, 78, 88
List systems, 3, 15, 115
Lloyd George, David, 8-9, 14
Loftus, S.D., 79, 91
Lubbock, Sir John, 3
Luce, Canon A.A., 32, 57
Lynch, Fionán, 37
Lynch, Jack, 59, 67-70, 72-82, 86-92, 125; on P.R., 67-8
Lyons, Dr. F.S.L., 8

132

133